John Black Johnston

Psalmody

John Black Johnston

Psalmody

ISBN/EAN: 9783337101879

Printed in Europe, USA, Canada, Australia, Japan

Cover: Foto ©Lupo / pixelio.de

More available books at **www.hansebooks.com**

AN EXAMINATION OF AUTHORITY

FOR

MAKING UNINSPIRED SONGS,

AND FOR

USING THEM IN THE FORMAL WORSHIP OF GOD.

BY

J. B. JOHNSTON,

PASTOR UNITED PRESBYTERIAN CHURCH, ST. CLAIRSVILLE, O.

"But in vain they do worship me, teaching for doctrines the commandments of men."—MATT. xv. 9.

ST. CLAIRSVILLE, OHIO:
JOHN STUART.
1871.

TO

THE MEMORY OF

MY DEARLY BELOVED

AND

VENERABLE FATHER AND BROTHER

IN

THE MINISTRY,

REV. JOHN T. PRESSBY, D. D.,

THIS LITTLE VOLUME

IS

VERY AFFECTIONATELY INSCRIBED

BY THE AUTHOR,

J. B. JOHNSTON.

St. Clairsville, O., May, 1871.

CONTENTS.

CHAPTER I.

PRINCIPLES PECULIAR TO THE ORDINANCE OF PRAYER EXAMINED, AS PRELIMINARY TO THE QUESTION INVOLVING THE ANALOGY OF PRAYER, PREACHING AND PRAISE.

What are the essential elements of prayer?—Human inability to pray—The spirit of prayer a grace of the Holy Spirit—This grace a promised blessing—Acceptable prayer is inspired—This inspiration explained and distinguished.. 17

CHAPTER II.

AN EXAMINATION OF THE ASSUMED ANALOGY AND PARALLELISM BETWEEN PRAYER, PREACHING AND PRAISE.

The assumption stated and questions examined—Scriptural elements of the ordinance of preaching the gospel—Principles of analogy applied—Scriptural elements of the ordinance of praise—Important distinctions applied—Parallelism found wanting.................. 23

CHAPTER III.

REVIEW OF THE DOCTRINE OF UNINSPIRED PRAYER, PRAISE AND PREACHING, AND THEIR ASSUMED PARALLELISM.

Review of a reviewer—Inspired and uninspired men placed in the same category—Divine inspiration and poetic genius in the same category—Authority of Divine inspiration weakened—Illogical comparisons—Mistranslations, paraphrases, etc., examined—Fallacy exposed—Absurd claims of Church prerogative—The Church passing on translations, or versions, not analogous to passing on Hymn-Books... 48

CHAPTER IV.

EXAMINATION OF SCRIPTURE AUTHORITY CLAIMED FOR MAKING AND USING, IN THE FORMAL WORSHIP OF GOD, UNINSPIRED SONGS.

In what we agree—In what we differ—Demand of negative proof unreasonable—In the true issue our brethren affirm—Five affirmative Proof-Texts for the Presbyterian system of Psalmody—Our friends argue both sides of the true issue—Irrelevant verbal criticism—Appeal to reason and argument from the "stronghold" texts—Authority from command—A representative paragraph examined—The leading point of assumption, its identities and deductions therefrom—The argument from Scripture example—Entrance into Jerusalem, Luke xix. 38 — "Pattern" for Presbyterian hymn-making—The second "pattern" case for so making, Acts iv. 24—Impromptu Prayer-meeting, or Committee on Revision of Bible Psalms—Commentators—Barnes and Jacobus—Reflections............ 81

CHAPTER V.

THE SCOTTISH VERSION OF THE BOOK OF PSALMS VINDICATED AS A TRANSLATION.

Importance attached to the question of translation—No other version subjected to such extreme criticism — Mistranslation defined — Charges of gross mistranslations examined—The First, the Sixteenth, and the Sixty-ninth Psalms vindicated from charges of gross mistranslation—Mistranslations in the prose Bible compared with the worst examples in Rouse—Charges of patchwork and paraphrase of Rouse examined—Manufactured patches charged to the account of Rouse—Specimens of similar and greater patches in our English version — Various classes of specimens—Use of Divine names, when not in the original, charged as a prejudice against Rouse—Superabundance of similar instances in our prose Bible..... 112

CHAPTER VI.

THE SCOTTISH VERSION COMPARED WITH THE SEPTUAGINT.

Why this comparison—Its importance in this discussion—The established opinion and decision of the Churches in regard to the Septuagint as a translation—Its defects compared with those of the

Scottish version—The claims of the Scottish version sustained by such comparison—Luther's translation incidentally noticed—Inferences.. 147

CHAPTER VII.

CONCLUSION.

The argument from history—Very briefly noticed—Of comparatively little importance in this controversy—Yet some facts of history with consideration—The Palatinate Churches—History not the rule of faith and worship—The mistake and its fatal consequences—Appeal to our readers—Address to brethren in the ministry—Appeal to the friends of union.. 157

INTRODUCTION.

WE have endeavored to explore the field of controversy, on the subject of psalmody, and to ascertain what are the true issues involved. The Presbyterian churches practically differ upon a vital question in relation to the matter of divinely instituted worship. This practical difference is the legitimate fruit of a difference, somewhere, in some fundamental principle; or there must be want of integrity to principle somewhere. The latter would be uncharitable, if directly charged, and must not be entertained. We misunderstand the subject, or we misunderone another. Perhaps there is misunderstanding in regard to both.

These are certainly very plain first principles common to the organic faith of all true Presbyterians, which, if consistently applied, would bind us all together in one practice in the formal worship of God. Here is a fundamental principle, regulating the Divine worship, to which we are all pledged, occupying a prominent place in the organic law common to us all—

"But the acceptable way of worshipping the true God is instituted by himself, and so limited by his own revealed will, that he may not be worshipped according to the imaginations and devices of men—or any other way not prescribed in the holy scripture." "But in vain do they worship me, teaching for doctrines the commandments of men."

Losing sight of these first principles, we soon diverge from the common line, and fall out by the way. It is high time that we were all, in this controversy, brought back to principles in common, and that we shape our discussions accordingly.

On the one hand, most of the treatises in favor of a scripture psalmody have been apologies for the Book of Psalms; or, defences of their use in the worship of God, to the exclusion of human compositions; or, their suitableness for worship in New Testament times; or, their superior excellence to all human songs. Most of these forms of discussion involve mere truisms—matter beyond legitimate debate among intelligent Christians. The Psalms of the Bible need no apology. They need no defence; since neither God, nor his works, nor his word need any defence. We make no attempt to show their fitness for the worship of God, or the authority for their use. God made them—fitted them for his praise, and commands us to sing. Treatises in the forms referred to are very well in their place. They are helpers of the faith of pious Christians who feed on God's word. Yet they may not meet the main points in this issue on the psalmody question.

On the other hand, our friends, in pleading their cause of a human psalmody, are very careful to avoid the discussion of first principles, and their application here; and the better to divert from the real question, demand of us authority for the *exclusive use of inspired songs*. About the authority to use the inspired songs of the Bible, there is not the shadow of dispute. No sane Christian holds that it is wrong to sing the songs of the Bible in the worship of God. Who, unless a pagan, or a turk, or an infidel, will refuse to sing, living or dying, the twenty-third Psalm? So far as inspired songs are concerned we all go together, by consent of all. What have we to affirm in debate here? What have we to prove? Surely not what no one denies. The matter of difference, of debate and proof lies elsewhere.

Our brethren diverge from the common way in which we all travel together in God's worship. They make their new songs, they worship with them, ask us to join them, affirming their authority for that new, and different and peculiar way of worship. Now are we called to prove our divine right to worship in a way our brethren affirm with us to be divinely authorized—a way in which they and we actually worship together? Or, is not the *onus probandi* theirs to carry, not ours? It is certainly very convenient, in this controversial discussion, to repeat the euphonious phrases, "The *exclusive system*," and to demand authority for the "*exclusive* use of *inspired songs*."

As our brethren invite us to follow them in their new way of making their own matter of praise, we hear, and weigh their assumed authority—for they *affirm* they have authority to make their own denominational hymns. We *deny*. Here, in a nutshell comprehension, is the whole field of controversy. There is no other. They have brought upon the stand their witnesses. We have heard the testimony; and have heard them sum up the evidence, and argue their case. Our work is to try their evidence in chief, cross-examine their witnesses, and review the whole argument. Nor are we to be diverted from this course by efforts to thrust upon us side issues, or false issues.

The friends of the Prayer-Book call on us to prove our authority for *exclusive* extempore prayer, and demand of us to show the wrong of *reading prayers*. Rome uses the wafer, calls on us to prove it wrong, and coolly demands the authority for the *exclusive use* of bread and wine, so of the hymn-book. Now we refuse to be decoyed by any such ambush. We have no text in our Bible that names either Wafer, Prayer-Book, or human Hymn-Book. Not one, saying they are wrong. Enough for us that their institution, as ways of worship, has no place in the Bible. It is their friends' business to find the institution there. Till that is done we shall be content to serve our Master in what we know to be his way, without wafer, prayer-book, or new hymnal.

The whole field of argument occupied by our brethren may be divided into the following sections:

1. The argument of assumption, of hypothesis and speculation, presented in the form of confident and complacent triumph, thus—

"If we may make our own prayers, and our own sermons, why may we not make the matter of our own praise?"

So long as the assumption here passes without challenge and investigation, our friends will seem to hold vantage ground. Here is assumed the very thing which should have been proved, before such illogical stride had been made to a conclusion remote from the premises. Are these parallelisms? Do the points of analogy warrant the assumption as true, the very matter to be proved? The fact that with our brethren, everywhere, this assumption seems to be used as unquestioned and unquestionable, has induced us to give it more elaborate consideration. We ask from our readers here, a patient, persevering and thorough investigation of all the principles involved.

2. The argument of high church prerogative—The Divine authority lodged in the Supreme Judicatory of the

church, to make and authorize church creeds, and on the same principle to make and authorize the matter of the church's worship. While it is conceded that no *man* has the right to prepare songs of praise to be used in the worship of God, yet it is presumed to be lodged with the "*church representative.*" By what authority does Rome declare the Pope infallible?—What the principle?

3. It is assumed that the command to *sing* Psalms, hymns and spiritual songs *implies* the authority to *make* the matter to be sung. The following three texts, it is assumed, furnish *authority* to *make* the songs: 1 Cor. xiv. 26; Eph. v. 17; Col. iii. 16. The two following texts furnish the example after which the *making* is to be performed: Luke xix. 38; Acts iv. 24. These are the "strong hold authority" for uninspired hymns.

4. The Scottish version is denounced in the form of attack upon Rouse, as mere "patch-work, paraphrase—no version at all." Rouse tried by another version, and not by the original text, and summarily condemned, it becomes an item of some importance, in the vindication of the truth, to give some attention to the subject, and settle the question in regard to the claims of the Scottish version to a place among recognized translations. Do we, as charged, sing uninspired Psalms while professing to sing inspired matter exclusively? It is our right to review this charge.

Where churches differ, and where their differences are the cause of their separation, nothing can be more important—the parties being equally honest—than to understand precisely the questions at issue. Parties may beat the air, and so exhaust their strength, while strengthening mutual prejudices, and their discussions fail to bring them any nearer to an understanding of the truth, and of one another. On the other hand, while the charges are rung upon the "want of fetters in the matter of praise in worship, as in preaching," we shall remain *in statu quo*, or in retrogression in regard to union.

Rouse's paraphrase—Rouse's party—Rouse's version, have nothing to do with the question of union here, so far as honest and intelligent men are concerned. Nor is it anywhere near this, where the issue lies, involving the question of union. It lies deeper, and is broader than this silly thing. If Rouse's version were thrown into the sea, the barrier stands intact in all its mountain largeness, since the songs of the Bible remain intact, and the distinction between the ordinance of praise and preaching stands marked in palpable lines on the pages of the Bible.

Sermons, infallible by divine inspiration, never was God's divinely appointed ordinance of preaching; but uninspired men, ordained and appointed to preach uninspired sermons, with specific directions to all hearers to bring them all to the test of the inspired standard—this is God's ordinance of preaching. God has given largely and abundantly inspired matter of praise—has commanded to sing, to *sing only*—and not one line in all his word suggestive of the thought, in regard to the duty or privilege of testing one line by the unerring standard of God's word, of all we may sing in his worship.

It is not a question in issue whether man, by divine ordination, may make and preach uninspired, fallible sermons. It is a question in issue whether it is God's work or man's to *make* the songs of praise with which God is to be worshipped. *This* is just the issue. To disabuse the mind of other issues, and bring to this, is the object of our feeble effort, in so far as this part of our work is concerned.

Believing that the divided worship of God, in all the churches, is the most decisive element *now* sundering evangelical departments of the household of faith, we have been induced to present this humble work for the consideration of union-loving Christians, whose creeds in regard to doctrine and order are substantially the same.

"Behold, how good and how pleasant it is for brethren to dwell together in unity." Zion's "watchmen shall lift up the voice; with the voice together shall they sing; for they shall see eye to eye, when the Lord shall bring again Zion."

CHAPTER I.

PRINCIPLES PECULIAR TO THE ORDINANCE OF PRAYER EXAMINED, AS PRELIMINARY TO THE QUESTION INVOLVING THE ANALOGY OF PRAYER, PREACHING AND PRAISE.

What are the essential elements of prayer?—Human inability to pray—The spirit of prayer a grace of the Holy Spirit—This grace a promised blessing—Acceptable prayer is inspired—This inspiration explained and distinguished.

THE salient point, the defiant argument for the use of a human psalmody, may be stated thus: As we make our own prayers and sermons, so may we make our own praise.

This assumes that prayer, preaching and praise are analogous, and present parallelisms. Now, if the assumption be true, the conclusion is logical, and the divine right of an uninspired psalmody is established.

We at once concede the divine appointment of extempore prayer without the book, and that we are not confined to the inspired prayers of Scripture. So, of the sermon. We concede the divine authority for uninspired extempore sermonizing. We are not confined in preaching to the inspired sermons of the Bible. Reading sermons from the Bible is not preaching at all, as Christ has commissioned an ordained gospel ministry.

To weigh fairly the argument of analogy here, we must distinctly define each of these ordinances, prayer, preaching and praise, and if their distinctions and discrepancies are more prominent than their analogies, then the argument fails. To this end we must have scriptural views of these ordinances, of their nature, their character and their essential elements.

Then, *what is prayer?* Not prayer in form merely; but, what is the prayer of God's appointment, which he hears and answers always? The prayer that God requires, that his promise recognizes and that he accepts, may be thus defined: Prayer is an offering up to God the desires of the heart, for things agreeable to his will, by faith in Christ, inspired and directed by the Holy Spirit. Such desires, offered thus to God, constitute prayer—not the prayer of the Pharisee, but of the publican.

To such prayer neither saint nor sinner is competent, without the special grace of the Divine Spirit implanting the desires offered. The sinner cannot be a fit *subject* of such desires. His unrenewed heart "is enmity against God, is not subject to the law of God, neither indeed can be." "The natural man receiveth not the things of the Spirit of God; for they are foolishness unto him; neither can he know them, because they are spiritually discerned." He can neither know nor feel spiritual want. He is spiritually dead. There is no breath in him.

The saint, by regenerating grace, is *made* the fit *subject* of spiritual desires. His new nature *can* entertain such desires. He is prepared to receive them, as the good heart to receive the seed of the word. Yet, this saint cannot pray without special grace—without the spirit of grace and supplication poured upon him by the Divine Spirit as the Author of prayer. "Likewise the Spirit also helpeth our infirmities; for we know not what we should pray for as we ought; but the Spirit, itself, maketh intercession for us with groanings which cannot be uttered. And he that searcheth the hearts knoweth what is the mind of the Spirit, because he maketh intercession for the saints according to the will of God." Saints are taught to say, in regard to prayer: "Teach us what we shall say unto him, for we cannot order our speech by reason of darkness." It is not in the power of a believer, even, to originate in his own heart an impulse producing a spiritual desire, and to breathe out that desire to God without the special influence of the Divine Spirit as the Author of prayer. That desire which constitutes prayer is the direct implantation of the Spirit, and beyond the originating power of the proper *subject* of such implantation, as Adam, when found a creature, was a proper *subject* for receiving and entertaining the breath of life, yet he could not breathe into himself that breath. The spiritual nature can *receive* and *entertain* the spiritual breathing, but the Spirit of God gives the breath the desire which is the essence of prayer.

THE SPIRIT, AS A SPIRIT OF GRACE AND SUPPLICATION, IS PROMISED TO MAKE SUCH PRAYER.

"I will pour upon the house of David, and upon the inhabitants of Jerusalem, the Spirit of grace and supplication." Zach. xii. 10. The Spirit helpeth our infirmities, making intercession for us with groanings—making intercession according to the will of God. The promises of the aid of the Spirit in making prayer are peculiar and distinguishing. In regard to aid in making hymns for the worship of God, there is no such promise. Dr Owen has well remarked—"It cannot be denied that the assistance which the Holy Spirit gives us, in our prayers and supplications, is more frequently and expressly asserted in the Scriptures than any other operation of his whatever."

THE PRAYER OF FAITH, ACCEPTABLE TO GOD, IS INSPIRED BY THE HOLY SPIRIT.

Inspiration should be defined, and carefully distinguished here. The term is so variously used there should be an understanding as to its use in this discussion. It is applied to poetic genius. This is the highest idea the Chinese have of inspiration. It is used of intoxicating liquors, and of almost all kinds of brain stimulants. It is used of the passions, anger, rage, love, etc. Most of these uses of the term are very figurative. It is applied to mere intellectual endowments, as Job—"And the inspiration of the Almighty giveth them understanding."

In all the instances noticed, the term inspiration is used in a loose, and improper sense. As the works of creation and providence differ materially, and yet are Divine works, so all these operations, which are called *inspiration*, present very *different* operations of the Divine Spirit. Creation brings from nothing into being. Providence sustains and controls what exists. Regeneration brings into being a new spiritual creature by creative power. Sanctification produces its appropriate changes upon its subject. There are inspirations which breathe into the mind new creations, as the breath of life was breathed into Adam. These are inspirations in the proper sense.

This sense of the term inspiration, which breathes new creations into the mind, by the Spirit, is its use applied to prayer and the Holy Scriptures. The one is the inspiration of *desires*. The other is the inspiration of *words*. The *words* of the Scriptures are inspired by the Holy Spirit. *This* makes them the veritable word *of God*, on the principle of *authorship*.

The question of the "*verbal inspiration*" of the Bible we will not here discuss. The reader may consult, for the defence of this cardinal truth, such standard works as Buck's Theo. Dic.; Brown, of Had., Dic. and Theo.; Dr. Scott's Com.; Prof. Dick's Theo.; Basis Union U. P. Church; Gaussen, of Geneva, etc.

The Scriptures state the doctrine of inspired prayer,

almost in explicit terms. "I called upon thy name, O Lord, out of the low dungeon. Thou hast heard my voice; hide not thine ear at my *breathing*, my cry." Lam. iii. 55, 56. Here Jeremiah calls his prayer, his *breathing*. "*My breathing, my cry.*" A breathing organism is chosen as the figure by which the Spirit illustrates prayer. A breathing organic frame is a proper *subject* of respiration. *It* breathes. It inhales breath. In this spiritual respiration of prayer, the only question around which a doubt can be thrown is this, viz.: By what power is the breath of prayer breathed into the soul, and the respiration sustained.

Then, whence the first impulse, in the heart, given to a gracious, spiritual and acceptable *desire* offered up to God, which he will answer as the prayer of faith? There can be but one of two answers properly entertained. Either, the *desire* in question receives its first impulse from the sinner himself, and so is self-willed and self-made; or, it is from the Spirit of God, and by him indited. Can there be any other conclusion? What other? Christ says, "Without me ye can do nothing." Without his power and providence, absolutely and universally, nothing. Without his Spirit and grace, spiritually and acceptably, nothing; each spiritual thing according to its kind, and according to the character of the grace promised—"grace for grace;" grace according to need; strength as the day is; for prayer according to our need, and the promise to supply that need. Is the breathing—the originating of acceptable *desires* in the heart an exception? Then, why the promises of the Spirit to do for us that very thing, without which the prayer of faith cannot be? To "*pour out a Spirit of grace and supplication.*"

And here, let it be borne in mind that there are no promises in the Bible, warranting aid in any other duty, like the promises in regard to prayer. None similar for *making* songs; none similar for making sermons, for teaching, for exhortation, for argument in defending truth. Here the promise secures groanings that we may not be able to utter—feelings of need, and desires we cannot express. How wonderfully strange—how distinguishing and peculiar the promises in regard to prayer!

Prayer, we conclude, is, therefore, *inspired*. It is not made by the will and power of the human heart. The Divine Spirit, according to his office and work, makes, by inspiration, the *desires* of the heart in prayer. Of these *desires* he is the Author, as he is the Author of the *words* in the inspired Scriptures.

CHAPTER II.

AN EXAMINATION OF THE ASSUMED ANALOGY AND PARALLELISM BETWEEN PRAYER, PREACHING AND PRAISE.

The assumptions stated and questions examined—Scriptural elements of the ordinance of preaching the gospel—Principles of analogy applied—Scriptural elements of the ordinance of praise—Important distinctions applied—Parallelism found wanting.

WE have, perhaps, said enough in the former chapter, in regard to how and by whom the matter of acceptable prayer is to be provided. Here, we think the Bible way is plain. The standing *office* and *work* of the Holy Spirit should remove all difficulty in the mind of every believing sinner. His office and work is to prepare prayers for all the saints as they are needed.

Doubtless, too, to the sincere Christian it is important to know the mind of the Spirit revealed in the word, in regard to the ordinance of praise. Not so much, however, in regard to the nature and duty of *singing* praise, simply. This is plain to all. About this there cannot well be any dispute whatever. He that runs may read. But how, and by whom, the songs of praise to be sung, are to be provided, that is not quite so plain to all. Indeed, *here* is the whole field of difficulty.

The following question is ever pressed as if sufficient to settle all doubts involved—"If we may *make* our own prayers, may we not *make* our own songs of praise, and offer them to God?" We answer—certainly, "*if*;" If *we may make our prayers*. But we see from the word of God we neither may nor can make our own prayers. That work belongs to the office of the Holy Spirit. He is engaged to do that work for us; and we think, that we poor sinners had better trust Him with it. And farther, as if it were the same—it is asked—"If we are not confined to the words of scripture in our prayers, why should we be confined to them in our praises?" So far from admitting the analogy assumed, we are bound by consistency to eject the idea of being confined in our prayers to any written *words* whatever. We are not confined to any written words, because the Spirit is promised to give us a knowledge and sense of our need, and inspire for us *desires* for supply. "Prayer is offering up our desires to God." Prayers read are unnatural—Prayers extemporized are the natural form of expressing the inspired feelings and desires and wants of the soul. The use of written words in praise is perfectly natural. Where, as an act of religious worship, was ever God praised by singing, without words written or recited? The use of extemporized songs in social praise is more unnatural than written prayers. The latter, alas! too often occurs. Where, when, how or by whom the former?

Still farther, on the assumed principle of analogy and parallelism, it is asked—"if, in the ordinance of preaching, we are not confined to the inspired words of the sermons recorded in the Bible, why, in the ordinance of social praise in the worship of God, confine ourselves to the use of the inspired songs of the Bible? Or, if we may *make* our own sermons—if we may use our own uninspired words in expounding the law and word of God, and in all our ministerial offers of Christ and his salvation to sinners, and in all our labors to persuade men to come to the Saviour, why not the same liberty in composing, penning and preparing hymns for the social praise of the church? These questions seem to be frank, and doubtless are deemed pertinent. Those who propound them seem also to believe them like mighty scales on whose equipoise hang very grave issues. Then let these questions be faithfully adjusted. In their adjustment we must bring them to the balances of the sanctuary. "To the law and to the testimony; if they speak not according to this word, it is because there is no light in them."

Doubtless it is important to understand all the principles involved in these test questions. We should know wherefore we preach. We should know the relation in which preaching stands to the Bible. Whether preaching the gospel by the ordained ministry, according to Christ's commission, be expounding or reciting the words of the Bible. We should know the extent of the commission to preach, as commanded and as illustrated by the preaching of Christ and his Apostles. So, doubtless, we should know wherefore we praise and wherefore we pray; and more— how we may secure, according to the will of God, the acceptable matter of all these. "How shall we order our speech before God," is the concern of every good man.

Now, in regard to preaching and praising, let us give a little attention—let us see just where we are. As for preaching, what is the rule? Are our sermons required to be inspired and infallible? Are the words of the sermon of Christ on the Mount, and the words of the sermons of any other, as recorded in the Bible, inspired and infallible? And may we search the Scriptures, as did the commended Bereans, to see whether those things spoken by Christ in that sermon on the Mount be so? May we try any of the sermons recorded in the Bible as the noble Bereans tried some sermons they heard preached? May we try the sermons written in the Bible as we may try with the Bible the sermons of Spurgeon, or any other preacher? Were those sermons heard by the Bereans, and by them brought to the test of the scriptures, of equal authority with the sermons recorded in the Bible, whether preached by Christ, or any other preacher? What were those sermons? And where are they now?

Again, it may be of some advantage here to inquire a little farther into the nature of the ordinance of preaching:—Would reading, or reciting the sermons preached by Christ, and by inspiration recorded in the Bible as a part of the written word of God, be an exemplification of the ordinance of preaching, and the fulfilment, in letter and spirit, of the gospel commission and command of Christ,—"Go ye into all the world and preach the gospel to every creature—teaching all nations to observe all things whatsoever I have commanded you?" Would the Bereans have been commended for bringing to the test of the Scriptures, which they searched, that kind of preaching?

This, now, brings fairly before us the following questions of practical importance to understand,—What is a faithful exemplification of the divine ordinance of preaching? And wherein have we a complete exemplification of the divine ordinance of praise?

In this connection, a passing remark only in reference to the second question—more hereafter in another. Paul says: "I will sing with the spirit, and I will sing with the understanding also." And he instructs the Colossians that their singing should be "with grace in their hearts." It may be noticed that the Apostle does not say he will make psalms, or any matter of praise. Nor, that he will make *and* sing. He does not direct the Colossians to make songs, or to sing songs made by some Christian brother—simply to *sing*. Could Paul have sung the twenty-third Psalm with the spirit and with the understanding? Could the Christians of Colosse have fulfilled the Apostles injunction to sing "with grace in the heart," by singing any Bible song? Would singing the songs in the Bible answer these specifications, and exemplify the ordinance of praise? If not, what essential element is wanting? Is it that the song should have been made by the singers themselves? Or that some poet should have made the songs for the occasions? Nothing of all these.

Again, as we are passing.—We have seen the Bible authority and institution for testing sermons by the scriptures as the Divine and permanent standard by which all preaching is to be tested. If the ordinance of praise in regard to "making" be parallel, then may we test the twenty-third Psalm, or any other Bible song by the scriptures? Can the scripture settle the question whether the songs of the Bible are *scriptural?* Does the Bible give any directions for testing the matter of the Psalms, hymns and spiritual songs it enjoins us to sing? Does it ever hint, even, that they may *not* be *scriptural?*—Or that they *should* be *scriptural?* For that would imply that they might possibly be *un*scriptural. The Bible warrants very distinctly the conclusion that sermons may be, and often are, *unscriptural.* It permits the conclusion, too, that *unscriptural* prayers may be made by good men even. Christ's disciples were not free from asking amiss. Nowhere in the Bible is there shadow of hint that the Christian in observing God's ordinance of praise, doing just what he requires, neither more nor less, can possibly sing *unscriptural* psalms, hymns or spiritual songs. If the thing were possible, why neither warning nor guard against it?

On the answers to the question propounded here, very much depends in the settling of the questions of an inspired psalmody, as also, of inspired prayers. To facilitate the satisfactory answering of questions proposed, a few more will be pertinent. Are we sure the same line of argument is applicable to the three different subjects of discussion here? That all stand or fall together? That the making of our own sermons, our own prayers and our own praises proceed upon the same principle of analogy, and present parallel cases? If so, then certainly we may make sermons just as the Apostles made them, to be thrown into the scripture crucible for trial by the noble Bereans; and so may we all make psalms and prayers to be subjected to the same fiery ordeal. For things, in their nature and from their institution necessarily rising no higher than *scriptural*, must stand subordinated to the standard of scripture.

SCRIPTURAL ELEMENTS OF THE DIVINE ORDINANCE OF PREACHING THE WORD.

The scriptural elements essential to the ordinance of preaching, will be found, even on slight examination, in the command and commission of Christ, the example of his own preaching—for here he was the perfect model who spoke as man never did—and in the examples of the Apostles, and their epistolary directions. Having here ascertained the essential elements of this Divine ordinance, we shall be able the more easily and safely to trace the analogy, and discover the parallel lines, if they can be found anywhere in all the scriptural elements essential to the ordinances of prayer and praise. The assumptions, in argument, of analogy or parallelisms, should be self-evident, or at least, nearly so, before we make them, and without attempt at proof, proceed to build argument upon them. It is very easy to say, or to write—"*if*," as in this issue—"*if* we may *make* sermons, we may *make* psalms." Are the cases parallel?—is the first thing in order, "*if*" we are seeking truth.

Christ gave commission to "go into all the world and

preach the gospel to every creature." "Teaching them to observe all things whatsoever I have commanded you." And Paul directing Timothy, says: "Preach the word." The words of Christ and Paul here, bear this construction —Go abroad, cry, proclaim by herald, speak to the people with the living voice. This command is explained by divine authority, Acts v. 20. "Go, stand and speak in the temple to the people, all the words of this life." This extempore speaking the gospel as a message of good tidings by herald, or voice of cries, is very distinctly exemplified in Christ's life and ministry. Here is the perfect model. "He came to Nazareth—and, as *his custom was*, he went into the synagogue on the Sabbath-day, and stood up for to read. And there was delivered unto him the book of the prophet Esaias." "And he closed the book, and he gave it again to the minister, and sat down. And the eyes of all them that were in the synagogue were fastened on him. And he began to say unto them, This day is this scripture fulfilled in your ears. And all bare him witness, and wondered at the gracious words which proceeded out of his mouth." Luke iv. 16–22.

In this very circumstantial narrative of Christ's preaching in the synagogue, we have, in detail, the scriptural elements of his own divinely appointed ordinance. Here we have the *time* set apart for the public ministrations of the gospel, the Sabbath-day. We have the *place* for the public ministrations of the Sabbath, and for the preaching of the word, the synagogue. Here was the place for the reading and expounding of the law, as was long the custom of the Jews. Here was an assembly of hearers convened to hear the word according to the order of the church. Here was the Book, the inspired Scriptures, which had been read and expounded by the ministry, time immemorial. Christ rose and opened that ancient roll.

The Book of God. In form he *read* his text, as it would seem, after he had announced "the place where it was written." It was the book of the prophet Esaias, and the subject of the text was himself. Having read aloud his text, he closed the book. In extempore address he expounded what he had read—the sermon was preached. If Christ's commands and example illustrate each other, as they do here, then we are authorized to understand his meaning is, when he says in his word—"Go preach to every creature," that we are to do as he did at Nazareth in the synagogue on the Sabbath-day; for he there preached the gospel. Then, obeying his command, and after his example, we should make the inspired word of God our text-book—should *read* that inspired word, and, according to the best of our ability, faithfully expound and apply its inspired teaching. Here we may notice that, when we preach according to Christ's commission and after his example, our text is certainly *inspired*, while our sermon is as certainly *uninspired*, is human and fallible and should be, by every hearer, brought to the test of the written and infallible word, and there tried as the noble Bereans tried the gospel sermons of Paul and Silas. Acts xvii. 11. Among all the elements of gospel sermons, according to the divine ordinance of preaching, inspiration or infallibility can find no place. Their highest attainments can reach no higher than *scriptural;* and then subordinated to the word, the only rule. So the commended Bereans judged of the preaching of the inspired Apostle of the Gentiles. Errors in preaching have a very ready corrective; since the church is well warned to be on her guard; and especially, since, of divine right, all have the unerring standard, and the example of the Bereans to use it as a test of every sermon heard.

The distinction betwixt the use of the so-called sermons

of the Bible, and the preaching ordained by Christ, by him exemplified, and by Apostles illustrated, is as broad as betwixt the reading and the preaching of the word. The use of the one is competent to all, saints and sinners, male and female, official and unofficial persons. The privilege and practice of the other are confined to the ordained ministry exclusively. This ordinance is limited in its administrations to those ordained by the laying on of the hands of the Presbytery, in the name of the head of the church, appointing to the work of preaching *uninspired* sermons, prepared by uninspired men, without extraordinary gifts. Their work is, nevertheless, subjected to the scrutiny of the humblest Christian, with the law and the testimony in his hand. Such is the character, and such is the *status* of the divinely appointed sermon preached by the ministry bearing Christ's commission.

Do we find in all this, and in divinely appointed praise and prayer a parallel? Do these all proceed upon the same principle? Is the same line of argument applicable to them all? Let us see—For here lies the pivotal point on which turns the whole issue involved in the question of a scripture psalmody. But let us again state the question,—"*If* we may *make* our own sermons, and must not confine ourselves to the very words of the inspired sermons of the Bible, may we not *make* the material of our own praises, and go outside of the Bible and gather composition for the one as for the other? Or—for we wish to meet fairly and fully the matter at issue—since *scriptural* sermons, fairly expounding God's law—since expositions unfolding the mysteries of the gospel infolded in the *inspired* Text-Book—since thus "*helping* the hope" of God's people, all exemplify the divine ordinance of preaching the gospel; why not our self-composed *scriptural* praises, as also our prayers, exemplify the ordinance of praise, and of prayer, as well?

We have noticed the scriptural views of inspired prayer, the scripture evidence on which such prayer is founded, and the promises securing such inspiration—the inspiration of *desires*. We have noticed the *verbal* inspiration of the Bible, the only inspiration for the ordinance of preaching. We have noticed that *all promises* in regard to the ordinance of praise, in fact, in spirit, in letter or in form, are confined to the *state of the heart in singing*. Or, perhaps, the attuning of the voice. What more?

Let us now trace a little the analogy, the parallelism, so confidently assumed—Let us carefully trace the principle and line of argument bearing upon the ordinances of preaching, praise and prayer—Let us apply the principle to the divine command assigning the duties in regard to these ordinances—Let us apply the principle to the material furnished by divine inspiration for each work, and to the promises of divine aid for the performance of the work assigned; for in all this we shall find the lines of Bible teaching clear and distinct. He that runs may read, and the wayfaring man need not err.

In regard to preaching sermons, the Text-Book, from which to preach, is furnished to the preacher by divine inspiration, is infallible, and cannot be the subject of promised aid. This Text-Book is to be preached. The charge is, "Preach the word." 2 Tim. iv. 2. "That, is the word of faith which we preach." Rom. x. 8. The *work* to which the preacher is ordained, is that for which he needs aid. That work embraces the reading and study of the Bible, to fit the better for expounding its teachings. This, too, includes rightly dividing milk and meat, to babes and strong men, each the portion according to the mind of the Master revealed in his word. Then the work proper, for which all other is preparatory, is the *discourse addressed* by the uninspired man, with the living voice to sinners in the Master's name. The sermon preached by the uninspired man, since it may not be *scriptural*, may, of divine right, be scrutinized and tested by the law and the testimony, so that every noble Berean may know whether the things spoken be so. Indeed, to every hearer, the command is, "Try the spirits." "For, the spirit of the prophets, must be subject to the Prophets." The work here, for which material is furnished, and aid promised, is perfectly plain. To encourage in this work the presence of the Master is promised, "Lo, I am with you always, even to the end of the world."

As the Head of the church provides something for all these ordinances, as his part of prayer, of praise and of preaching, and in each requires of us something to be done, may we do God's part, or leave ours undone? May we interfere with his prerogative, reserved to himself and delegated to none, in these divine ordinances? May we go beyond his appointment in either of these? If he has made psalms, hymns and spiritual songs, and given them to us to be sung; and has given us no encouragement, in any form, by command or promise, of help, to do what he has done, viz.: Make songs for us to sing, and has commanded us to sing them, and nothing more, what is our work, evidently, in this ordinance? Since we are here examining analogies, let us see God's part in prayer: May we reject the Spirit's work and indite our own prayers? May we reject the mediation of Christ, and ask in our own name? May we, instead of confining ourselves to the promises, ask what we please and as we please?

In regard to the observance of the ordinance of praise, what is the *work* to which every worshipper is called? What is the *material*, by Divine inspiration, furnished by the Head of the church for every worshipper? And what is the *aid* promised to every worshipper to qualify for the proper use of the material provided, and for the acceptable performance of the *duty required?*

With these questions before our minds, and the answers suggested by the analogy of faith, we shall be better prepared to answer some others.

Does the ordinance of praise *require*, or even contemplate, the composing, penning, making of songs, the material for praise either for ourselves, for others, or for the use of the church? Is *every* worshipper called to this *work*, as to the work of prayer, so that to omit it is to sin? Is *any* worshipper so commissioned to this *work?* Is the church collective, in her courts, called to this *work?* Has *any* worshipper a promise of aid in this *work*, as in prayer, and as in a work to which he is *called?* Have *all* worshippers such promise? Have church judicatories such promise? How is it? Does any one single promise, directly or indirectly, expressly or impliedly, secure aid and encouragement in *this work?*—In making songs for praise as in making sermons to preach? True, there may be some analogy, or parallelism betwixt the *text*—the inspired word from which the *sermon* is to be framed, and the *song* God made and gave and appointed to be *sung* to his praise. As also, a parallelism betwixt the *preaching* of the sermon, which is the preacher's *work*, and the *singing* of the song, which is the worshipper's *work* of Divine appointment. God is the Author of both *Text* and *Psalm*. The preacher and worshipper, by the help of God, perform both the *preaching* and the *singing* as their appropriate and Divinely appointed work. And more—to both these works there is a call imperatively binding on the called to perform, each his work; with a woe also on all who fail to meet the obligation. For both these works there is need of aid from God; and both these are ordinary duties for which God furnishes ordinary qualifications. For both these duties aid is promised; aid for making and preaching sermons; aid for singing praise. But, no aid promised or expected by any one for making a text-book, for the Sacred Canon is closed and all inspiration of books closed with it, and all work for which inspiration was ever given is closed also. No aid is either promised or expected for making Hymn-Books more than any other books scribblers may choose to make; inspiration for that work having been closed, and that work withdrawn from the church also. Where then, the analogies, the parallelism? Where the parallelism for warranting the challenge—"If we may *make* our own sermons, may we not *make* our own psalms?"

That there is promised aid to the ambassador of Christ in the preaching of the gospel, needs no further argument. This may here be safely assumed as conceded by all. It remains but to notice the fact that, in regard to worship, all promised aid is for the *work* of *singing*, none for the work of hymn-making. Here there is no need of extended argument. If God commands his people to *do*, he promises aid for that work required. For, "who goeth a warfare any time at his own charges?" 1 Cor. ix. 7. "And as thy days, so shall thy strength be." Deut. xxxiii. 25. This is not matter of debate. Christ furnishes promised material beyond our resources for every work to which he calls us; and all the aid needed in using that material. Is it not strange that—on a certain assumed hypothesis—there is not one single promise to aid in hymn-making, nor even a remote allusion to such a duty, work or privilege even, in all the Bible? Is it so of any other work, duty, calling, privilege in regard to the worship of God? The conclusion is forestalled. Christ calls none, authorizes none, privileges none to prepare songs for the use of praise in his church. This was a work equal to inspiration—equal to a God; and to men it cannot be *comely*. These truths, next to self-evident, none will, or should controvert. Indeed, the highest assumption of any opponent known, is that psalm-making is a mere privilege—a Christian liberty in which any poet may indulge. And this whole matter of privilege merely inferential; and that, too, in the matter of the worship of God. A liberty which may be enjoyed at will, or may never be exercised. A liberty, of course, involving no one enjoying it in any responsibility, duty or obligation whatever. A Christian liberty and privilege entirely "*sui generis*"—none such known among all the Christian privileges guaranteed to fallen sinners. Or, if this conclusion be not accepted—if it be admitted that privilege does involve corresponding obligation—then it must follow that every one, whose Christian privilege it is to make psalms for the worship of God, in the ordinance of praise, is involved in the obligation. It is the privilege of every minister of the gospel to make and to preach sermons; and woe to that privileged minister who will not preach the gospel. It is the privilege of every Christian to observe the ordinance of prayer, secret, social and public; and woe to that Christian who will never bow the knee in prayer to God. It is the Christian privilege of every one enjoying divine revelation, and divinely prepared songs, with the right use of reason and his senses, to sing God's praise in his worship; and woe to that privileged sinner who will not sing psalms in the praise of God, and so worship him. Then, here is the parallelism—the making and preaching of sermons by all who are privileged to preach; and the singing of God's praise by all whose privilege it is to sing. Here are the parallel lines; not the *making* of *sermons* and *making* of *psalms*.

Then, the parallel stands thus—God has given the sermon-maker an inspired text-book out of which to make sermons. He has also given the church a book of inspired praises to be used for praising him; not to be used for making a book of praises. He has commissioned and commanded the preacher to make, with reading and study, and preach sermons of his own and uninspired. This is his work. He has commanded his whole church—he has commanded all saints and sinners, too, to sing psalms to his praise as the work of all. Thus we find the analogies, the parallels, and the absence of them. Who ever tested the Book of Psalms—which all of right may sing—by the scriptures, which every sinner may apply as the test of every sermon heard.

Before closing this chapter on parallelisms, a word farther in regard to the essential and distinguishing elements of the divine ordinances of prayer and praise—the false assumptions and the conclusions therefrom consequently false.

Prayer has, for its very first creative and impulsive power, the inward operations of the Holy Spirit in the originating of the *desires* of the heart. As in regeneration, the Spirit *creates* a spiritual *being*, so in prayer, *He creates* spiritual *desires*. This creation of spiritual desires identifies with the operations of the Spirit in awakening into active exercise the graces of the soul, as faith, love, hope; of which the Spirit is the Divine Author. Now, this inward impulsive power of the Spirit shapes and controls, and gives direction to all the desires of the heart, and all the exercises of the graces without the intervention of external objects addressing the mind through the external senses. We have no need for the use of the eye in prayer; we close it, as if we felt its use hurtful to the exercise of the inward spiritual graces of the soul. We, for the same reason, have no need of *The Book*, nor of its

4

word-signs as objects of sense to lead the mind, and choose for it the matter of its exercises. If ever there can be need for the use of *The Book*, in prayer, it must be in social prayer. But here the Spirit alone can give "*one accord in prayer and supplication.*" This "*accord*" is secured by promise, else how could there be social prayer acceptable to God without "*The Prayer-Book?*" Pentecostal times illustrate the nature of the ordinance of prayer, and the promise of the Spirit in giving "*one accord*" to the desires of many hearts in social prayer. And just here we see the fitness of previous agreement for concerted prayer. Matt. xviii. 19.

These views of the nature of prayer, and of its essential elements, finding no parallel in the nature and ordinance of praise, lay a solid foundation for unanswerable argument against "*The Prayer-Book.*" For prayer and the book before the open eye are about as congenial as "*vinegar upon nitre.*"

The principle in praise is entirely reversed, as really so as the locomotive is reversed by the hand of the engineer on the lever, reversing the operations of the motive power, and evolutions of the entire rotary machinery of the engine. The mode of the mental and spiritual operations in praise is changed. The mind here, with all its intellectual and active powers, is controlled by *outward forms* of things addressed to the outward senses, the eye or the ear, and through these to the understanding and the heart. Here the eye, *The Book*, and its *words* form the *media* and essential element of praise. Essential to social praise; since to sing with "one accord" God has ordained and given *The Book*—for how can we sing without it? The very first mental and spiritual operation in the mind of the worshipper is produced with the *sight* of the *words* of the song stereotyped, and in the *Book*, before the eye, or read out from the book, and falling upon the ear, through sense to the understanding, and then to the *heart;* not as in prayer, which has its *beginning in the heart*, where praise *ends*. In praise, *words* in the *Book* are signs of ideas. Ideas are the images formed in the mind by the words, as forms or types reflecting from the Psalm its thoughts, sentiments, truths, as the mind of the Spirit, through this medium, addressed to the understanding of the worshipper. In singing praise the mind is *led*, in all its powers, and in all their operations—not, as in prayer, with outward senses closed to all objects of sense—but, by tangible and visible things, acting upon the mind as a mirror throwing back, by its reflections, the images of things, from without into the soul. The soul, in its exercise in praise, must closely *follow* the object before the eye just wherever that visible moving object *leads* the *eye*— from verse to verse, from line to line, from word to word, and from thought to thought as the Spirit of the Lord *leads by the words of the song, in The Book.* Here, all the feelings of the heart of the worshipper must be in correspondence with the *words* of the song, *in the book*, put into the mouth, and the sentiments of the song indited by the Spirit put into the heart. The words make, or frame, the heart with which we praise. In prayer, the inspired heart makes, or frames, the words with which we worship.

Here, indeed, is a parallelism; but not where our friends, over the way, desire to find it. It is here. God's Spirit of inspiration has something to do by way of inditing in both cases. The Holy Spirit, in prayer, indites the *thoughts* sent from the heart in *words*. These *words* must be subordinated to the inward inspiration of *desires*. The same Spirit, in praise, indites the *words* of the song, which command corresponding *thoughts* within, formed by the images of the *thoughts* of the Spirit in the inspired words. Images, or ideas, in the heart must here correspond to their forms in the Book. Instead, therefore, of making our own prayers, and our own praises as well, we neither can nor may make either. In the one case the Spirit *has*, by inspiration, *made* abundantly. In the other, the Spirit is promised *to make* by inspiring desires as needed for use. And this is the standing office and work of the Spirit in the church. Then, here we have another parallelism suggested, not suiting our friends, however: If we need inspiration, or inditing in the matter of prayer, why not in praise?—and with all the difference here in our favor; for prayers amiss are temporary, and may pass away, but hymns amiss are repeated, fixed in the book, and become the standing error of the church. If we must worship with *The Book*, let it be inspired.

Another view of our friend's parallels—If making and using psalms, prayers and sermons, as assumed, proceed on the same principle, and on the same form of authority; since the command to sing, to pray, to preach implies to make sermons, prayers and psalms; then, we are to make prayers and psalms impromptu and extempore alike, and without the Book, as our friends tell us psalms were made and used, Luke xix. 38, and Acts iv. 24. This proves too much. Our friends will make, with pen, the hymns they use, and book them. Yet they "*fight against the Prayer-Book.*" Why? Sure, Holy Mother books both! Which is right? Or do parallels diverge sometimes?

Again: If the command to *sing* implies authority to make the psalms, and to prepare a written manual for standing use in praise, as is done upon this same assumed authority, just as the command to preach implies authority to make sermons, then this will follow: If we may make and use a written Hymn-Book, we may make and use a written Prayer-Book, we may make and use a written Sermon-Book. Then, like *Rome* and *England*, we may sing from the Book, pray from the Book, and preach from the Book. Perhaps *Mass* as well. Things equal to the same, are equal to one another. If praise be equal to preaching and prayer, then preaching and prayer are equal to praise. So Rome books them all. And Roman logic is right!

Once more: Each of these ordinances, as regards their administrators, has, in addition to the command and commission, specific *instructions* for fulfilling the commission, and obeying the command. And just here is where our brethren stumble and miss their way; for just here lies all the world of difference. In each case we have *first*, the commission and command for the work. Then, to each is added specific instructions suited to the peculiar work. For each work the man of God is furnished and perfected by his special instructions. These instructions differ just as the nature and duties and work of these ordinances differ. The instructions of the one differ from the other, as the instructions of a Minister to one Foreign Court may differ from the instructions of a Consular Agent to some other.

These specific instructions are all, more or less, as the nature of the work requires, exemplified by Christ, his Apostles, Prophets, etc. From instructions exemplified we easily *prove* that these three ordinances are not parallel. Each so differs from the others, as to prove that Psalms must be written and booked, and that the others must not be. They prove that Psalms are inspired and given in the Book. They prove that prayer is inspired, but given in the heart, and may be unutterable. They prove that sermons are not inspired, either for heart or book; but uninspired and extempore. Such are implied in the exemplified instructions for the scriptural administrations of these ordinances. Let these instructions be all carefully studied, as they must be before this question will be settled.

We ask a hasty glance, only, at these very instructive instructions.

First, Instructions given to all commissioned to administer these ordinances. For preparing and preaching sermons they are ample. "Give attendance to reading." "Meditate upon these things." "Shun not to declare all the counsel of God." "A workman that needeth not to be ashamed, rightly dividing the word of truth." "Strive not about words." "Shun babblings." "Avoid unlearned questions." "In meekness instructing those that oppose themselves." No end here—Details are so ample and so specific, chapters might be written without repeating specifications in the bill of instructions, as found in the Bible. All this, too, suggestive of the fact of the weakness and fallibility of those bearing the commission; and, consequently, the propriety of bringing all their administrations to the standard. The treasure is committed to earthen vessels—men of like passions—men who, from the best specimens of their class, give evidence of the need of instructions, and of authorized test of their ministrations. Peter was withstood to the face, because he was to be blamed. Paul and Barnabas fell out by the way; and when not inspired, it was possible for them to err.

So of prayer. In how many forms are we cautioned of the danger of praying amiss? Here, too, space forbids extended specifications. How significant this prayer— "Lord, teach us to pray." Christ did teach *how* to pray. He has given examples both for warning and for instruction. The Pharisee's prayer. The long prayers of this sect. The prayer of the mother of Zebedee's children. Then the publican's prayer. The prayer of the thief on the cross. The importunate widow. Jacob's wrestling. But where end, with instructions for the ordinance of prayer? Then again—How to know that our prayers are of the Spirit's inditing. Here, too, are Bible instructions for testing. The will of God revealed, according to which the Spirit implants *desires* in the heart.

Secondly, A glance, as we pass, at the ample instructions to *hearers*, for the testing of sermons and prayers. If the Divine instructions to hearers required implicit faith and obedience in everything preached—if there was not a single hint that sermons might be questioned or challenged, might not this silence be suggestive, at least, of an inference that they might be inspired; or, like papal bulls, be received as infallible? Far otherwise are all the facts here. Every line of instruction to the people suggests the fallibility of every preacher, and of every sermon. Bear with us a little here, in reviewing the copious and specific instructions given—the masses need them.

"Take heed how ye hear," calls up, in the very preface to instructions, the idea, not only of subjective scrutiny, but objective, as well, in regard to the sermons heard. "Search the scriptures," not only for eternal life, but to become skilled Bereans, not easily carried away by winds of doctrine. "Try the spirits," because the spirits of the prophets may not be subject to the prophets, as they ought, and, therefore, their sermons found wanting. Thus we might proceed, and fill pages with references of this kind. There is still a more distinct and impressive form of instructions—

Thirdly, Commended example. The Bereans "were more noble, in that they received the word with all readiness of mind, and *searched the scriptures daily, whether those things were so.*" These noble Bereans, applying the instructions for hearing, as in duty bound, searched the scriptures daily to know whether the sermons, preached by the inspired Paul and his companion Silas, were in accordance with the only infallible rule by which all sermons should be tried by every hearer. These Bereans never tested, by the rule, the *inspired epistles* of the man whose sermons were put to such rigid scrutiny. Nor were they ever known to have thus tested their hymnology.

The whole Bible is full of instructions to hearers of sermons, all demonstrating that the character of the essential elements of the ordinance of preaching presents almost a contrast to the character of the matter of praise as recognized in the specific instructions in regard to this ordinance. Of the ordinance of prayer, the same things are substantially true as of preaching. Prayer may be amiss. Of such, example is not wanting. We have much instruction in regard to true prayer, and many examples illustrating the character of the prayer God hears. We have abundant instructions *how* to pray, and how to know whether our prayers have the Spirit for their Author. Chapters might be written on the subject of *instructions* for *testing sermons* and *prayers*. O, how fallible must our sermons be at best! And, O, how much our very tears and prayers need washing! How much does that man know of the evil of sin; of the depth of human depravity; of the deceitfulness of the heart; of our proneness to err, who cannot see the need of *instructions how to make* and to *try sermons* and *prayers*, on the ground that they may be poor, feeble, erring, deluding, dangerous things?

Fourthly, Here the inquiry is forced upon us—How of praise? Have we instructions here? For what? To what confined? Is everything plain here? Is everything just parallel to the instructions in regard to *preaching* and *prayer?* Ample instructions for *singing*—*what* to *sing*, and *how* to *sing*. All just as plain as in the matter of *making sermons, preaching* them, *hearing* them, *testing* them by the rule. We are instructed to *sing* psalms, hymns, songs, just as we are instructed to *read* and *search* the scriptures. We are instructed to *sing* with the voice. We are instructed to *sing* with the understanding, which implies the use of means to know the meaning of the matter we sing—perhaps by our own prayerful study, and with the help of the ministry. We are instructed to *sing* with the heart, and to make melody in the heart to the Lord. How ample the instructions in regard to *singing!*—ample, as to *preaching* or to *prayer*. He that runs may read. And why all this specific instruction in regard to *preaching, praying* and *singing?* These are cardinal ordinances. God is jealous of his own institutions, and of his worship. Another inference irresistible—*sermons, prayer* and *singing may be amiss*, and, therefore, the line upon line and the precept upon precept here.

Besides this, a *fifth fact* is suggested here in connection with the questions above: In addition to the total *want* of *instruction* for *making* and *preparing matter* of praise, there is neither *command* to make psalms for praise, nor *promise* of grace, or aid, in any form, for such work, nor the shadow of either available on the part of *any man*, of *any church*, of *any supreme judicatory*.

These *facts* and *inquiries* force upon the mind corresponding and logical *conclusions*—conclusions from which there is no evasion. They do shut us up to *one* or the *other* of the following: either,

1. It matters not *what* we *make* for *praise* in the worship of God, or *what* we sing; for, in the absence of all instructions in regard to the *matter*, or *making* of song, we are without law, and cannot transgress. "Where there is no law there is no transgression." It is the same to God what psalms, hymns and spiritual songs we sing, and a matter of indifference who made them. This deduction lies necessarily at the foundation of the system of all uninspired hymn-making and singing in the formal worship of

God. This is essential to the New Testament Christian liberty claimed—a liberty to *make* and *sing*, according to our creed and conscience, in the absence of all restrictions. The practice of the churches, and their defenders confirm this conclusion. For, if the churches may make their hymnology a part and form of their creed, then it is in their own hands to be shaped according to their respective faith and taste. The hymns of the Calvinist, the Armenian, the Arian, the Universalist, the Catholic, the Mormon—all alike to God—for, he permits all to make and sing what they please, without shadow of condition or restriction; if heart be right and music good, God is satisfied, and man is pleased.

That our brethren choose this horn of the dilemma, and boldly face the consequences, is proved by their own church deliverances, and the endorsed vindications of their doctrine and practice on the subject of psalmody. They can consistently sing what they denounce as gross error—and they do. Proof—

They have denounced the Scottish version of the Book of Psalms, as teaching, "very serious doctrinal and historical errors;" as teaching "gross errors;" as teaching what "leads directly to the error of *sinless perfection*;" as teaching what "utterly subverts the doctrine of atonement, by representing the blessed Saviour as a forced victim to Divine justice;" as teaching the doctrine, "that the *soul* goes down into the grave with the body;" as teaching "that the human soul of our blessed Lord was thus buried with his body."

And, yet, the version of the Psalms so charged, and the charges endorsed by Doctors of Divinity, by Theological Professors, by ecclesiastical bodies, venerable Synods, etc., has the sanction of the supreme judicatory—is sung in many, and may be lawfully sung in all of their churches.

They choose the position that it is Christian liberty to sing whatever supreme judicatory may please to sanction, truth or error. So they have done, so they still do. It is not essential that their hymns be evangelical. If their hearts be right, the words matter little. And if the heart be bad, as the Arians', it alters not, materially, the matter to sing a Bible Psalm.

Why might we not as well dispense with word singing altogether? Why not just sing with sound unmeaning?— and with heart warmed by sound of music inspiring? Is it not moving that way fast enough? Perhaps, just held in check enough to save from shattering the machinery organic. If this *first* conclusion, with what logically follows, be inadmissible, there is *one* other.

2. God, himself, having amply provided, by infallible inspiration, Psalms, Hymns and Spiritual Songs, to his own mind and after his own heart, has made no provision for any other. These need no instruction for testing, and consequently have none. Therefore, all this silence here— no command to make—no instructions for making—no instructions for examining—no promise or encouragement in regard to any such work—demands, if the *first* conclusion be ejected, the acceptance of the *second*. Will our friends suggest any other possible? If they cannot, and the dilemma has but *two* horns, which will they choose?

And now, in concluding this chapter, may we *make* our own psalms, as we *make* and *preach* our own sermons? If we perch upon the *first* horn, certainly. If on the *second*, we shall cling to the songs of the Bible. To God, the Judge, we leave the rest.

CHAPTER III.

REVIEW OF THE DOCTRINE OF UNINSPIRED PRAYER, PRAISE AND PREACHING, AND THEIR ASSUMED PARALLELISM.

Review of a reviewer—Inspired and uninspired men placed in the same category—Divine inspiration and poetic genius in the same category—Authority of Divine inspiration weakened—Illogical comparisons—Mistranslations, paraphrases, etc., examined—Fallacy exposed—Absurd claims of Church prerogative—The Church passing on translations, or versions, not analogous to passing on Hymn-Books.

A VERY confident writer, whose issue is perhaps the latest on this subject, 1866, writes thus: "The Reviewer proposes a false issue, when he asks, 'Where has God authorized any *uninspired man* to prepare songs of praise for the church?' Presbyterians answer, nowhere! Our doctrine is, that individuals may employ the noble poetical talents, with which the 'Author of every good and perfect gift,' has endowed them in composing hymns, agreeably to the example in Acts iv. 24, of a song of praise gathered partly from Ps. 2, and partly from other portions of the sacred records. But 'to prepare these Psalms for the church,' is not the prerogative nor the privilege of 'any uninspired man,' which Dr. P— insinuates to be the Presbyterian doctrine. This is the province of the church herself, as represented by her supreme judicatory. She examines, and, where found needful, *amends* these productions, and then issues her sanction to their adoption in public worship, just as the Scottish General Assembly sanctioned Rouse. But, replies Dr. P—, 'There is no promise of the influences of the Holy Spirit to assist *any man* in preparing these Psalms.' But, are there not precious and abundant promises to THE CHURCH OF CHRIST, that the presence of the Holy Spirit shall be with her in her public councils? Has he not promised to be with her 'to the end of the world?' And have we not at least as good grounds to hope for this gracious presence with the collective 'body of Christ,' when the church is amending and authorizing these songs of praise, as when uninspired men are *explaining* Rouse to their congregations, and putting into their hearts the sentiments which they shall feel when uttering the language of the paraphrase?" Pp. 132, 133.

Our apology for making this long quotation, is that it contains, in a nut-shell scope, the sum of volumes of this same kind of " darkening counsel by words without knowledge;" and we avail ourselves of its comprehension. It presents one of the strong pillars reared for the sustaining of the whole fabric of a human psalmody; if this falls, no other prop can sustain it. This specimen of forcing conclusions from premises where there is no logical relation, or analogy, so strikingly exemplifies the whole course of argument for uninspired hymns and prayers, we wish to have it before us, and before the eye of the reader, so as to see at once the full strength of the opponent. Let us then, carefully look at some of the main points of argument sup posed to be in the quotation before us.

FIRST, INSPIRED AND UNINSPIRED MEN ARE PLACED IN THE SAME CATEGORY, IN OFFICIAL CALLING AND WORK.

It is distinctly conceded, in the quotation above, that "*Nowhere*, has God authorized any *uninspired man* to prepare songs of praise for the church." Now, this is very well because it is true. But has it any kin to the next statement? "Our doctrine is that individuals may employ the noble poetical talents with which the 'Author of every good and perfect gift' has endowed them"—uninspired men here of course—" in composing hymns, agreeably to the example in Acts iv. 24, of a song of praise gathered partly from Ps. 2, and partly from other portions of the sacred records." That is, what Luke did, Acts iv. 24, the Christian poet may do. But Luke composed a hymn just as any Christian poet may. And as Luke did no more, and no less, than other inspired writers of songs, so every Christian poet may do, what any inspired poet did in writing the inspired songs of the Bible. What David, Asaph, Ezra, Luke did in composing and penning songs inspired, and recorded in the Bible, the *un*inspired Christian poet may do. Whatever we may justly claim for our divinely inspired poets in the matter of composing praise to be sung in the worship of God, the Christian poet, *un*inspired, may claim. Inspired men have quoted, expounded and applied the Book of Psalms; and have "gathered from other portions of the sacred record;" they have expounded and applied these gatherings; they have incorporated these gatherings and expositions with the other canonical books, all by the unquestioned authority of the head of the church, and by the infallible inspiration of the Holy Spirit. To this very work they were divinely called; for this work they were divinely qualified; in this work they were divinely and infallibly guided. To do this work, to which called, was not only their Christian privilege and liberty, but their incumbent and imperative duty, about which they could have no choice, and from which they could not, on peril of condemnation shrink. Such was the official work, to which Luke was called in penning Acts iv. 24. And so of all the inspired writers of song, whose penmanship is found in the Bible. Now, what is the claim made for the *uninspired*, but otherwise gifted, Christian poets? Let us, from the same author, see :—

"Presbyterians plead for the use of the songs of inspiration, just as the Apostles used them. For example, THERE IS NOT A SOLITARY INSTANCE IN THE NEW TESTAMENT OF THE SINGING OF THE PSALMS OF DAVID IN A LITERAL FORM. On the contrary, the Apostles used the Book of Psalms in quite a different mode, in the only *two* cases in which they employed them in social praise. One of these is Luke xix. 38. The disciples took part of a verse from Ps. cxviii., but sung it with alterations adapted to their circumstances. The *second* case is in Acts iv. 24. The beginning of second Psalm is sung by Peter, John, and their company, then an addition, in the beginning, then a narrative of what David spoke, then an application to Herod, Pontius Pilate, etc., then an enlargement by considering the hand of God in the whole, and finally the song concludes with desires suited to their circumstances. This is an inspired pattern for making new Testament Psalms. It groups together parts of the Psalms along with other inspired matter, *just as* Dr. Watts and Presbyterians do." Pp. 79, 80.

Is it not true in logic, as in philosophy, that, "things equal to the same are equal to one another." "Dr. Watts and Presbyterians,"—that is, the uninspired poets—"have no authority to prepare songs of praise for the church." "It is the province of the church herself as represented by the supreme judicatory." Yes, and "to examine, and, where found *needful, amend* these productions, and then issue her sanction to their adoption in public worship." But the authority of Luke being *equal—just as* Dr. Watts, etc."—to the authority of poets; and the authority of the poets *equal* to the authority of Luke, in composing Acts iv. 24, and Luke xix. 38, consequently neither the productions of the poets, nor the compositions of Luke the physician, are authorized to be sung till the supreme judicatory of the church " issues her sanction for their adoption in public worship, *just as* the Scottish General Assembly sanctioned Rouse." This placing in the same category the poetic works of Luke, and the other inspired poets, is about as logical as the Jew plowing with an ox and an ass. The *inspired* Luke and other *inspired* Psalm-makers, might demur here against this unequal yoking with *uninspired* scribblers. The animals are not just alike. Nor are the products of their pens just alike. But it is some relief to the uninspired poets and to the argument of the quotation—whether to Luke and the other inspired poets we say not—that the church prerogative comes in with its interposition. The "supreme judicatory" can clothe the ass with an ox-hide!

Seriously—can that course be a good one, and its defence scriptural, that requires the calling, the authority, the place, the work of an inspired writer to be placed in the same category with the work of uninspired poets? The work of inspired poets of no more authority than the productions of uninspired men? And do the inspired songs of the Bible stand in the same relation, of authority, to the church, to her judicatories, etc., and to all her worshippers, that the poetical compositions of the poets do, having no authority to be sung, till authorized by the supreme judicatory of the church? God inspired holy men to write songs of praise, to place those songs in the Bible, as a part of the sacred canon, as God's word; yet they were not "*prepared for* the church," since "this is the province of the church herself, as represented by her supreme judicatory." She *examines, amends, sanctions* their *adoption* in public worship." "This is an an inspired pattern for making New Testament Psalms. It groups together parts of the Psalms along with other inspired matter *just as* Dr. Watts and Presbyterians do." Luke and Watts "employ the noble poetical talents with which the 'Author of every good and perfect gift' has endowed them in composing hymns, as Luke in Acts iv. 24." After examination—amendment—("*if needed!*") sanction by the church, Luke and Watts might use one another in public worship! A curious query springs upon us here. Did Luke sing Acts iv. 24, in worship before his composition passed the "supreme judicatory of the church?"—"*just as Dr. Watts?*" Did David, Asaph, Isaiah, Luke, and with them the church, sing their inspired songs, with or without, the sanction of the "supreme judicatory of the church," or, by the simple authority of God to sing them? Let us hear what our author says in answer to this question: He can argue either side—Hear the other:

"It is a plain dictate of common sense, that to versify such passages of the other scriptures, as Isa. xii. is no more 'to make songs of praise' than to versify the one hundred and fifty Psalms after the manner of Rouse. Such sublime and beautiful portions of the sacred records are songs of praise *already made*, and whether they be found in the New or the Old Testament, they are admirably suited to the worship of God. But is it lawful to use them in praising God? What says the Holy Ghost by the writers of many of those passages? 'Sing unto the Lord'— 'In that day (gospel day) shall THIS song be sung'—' Sing unto the Lord a new song.' (Isa. xlii. 10)—But we think the *authority* of Isaiah is quite sufficient if there were no other." Pp. 140, 141.

And now, will this author, or any one else plead that— like Watt's, or other *uninspired* poets' productions—"The song of Miriam, of Moses, of Deborah, of Barak, of David, of Asaph, of Isaiah, of Luke, of Peter, John and their company," are not "*already made*," or prepared for worship, but must pass the examination and sanction of "supreme judicatory? The authority of inspired and uninspired poets to prepare praise for the use of the church in the worship of God, is *just as* unlike as *authority* and *no authority*. The authority of inspired poets, and the authority of supreme church judicatory, in the business of preparing songs of praise, for the use of the church, in the worship of God, are *just as* unlike as *authority* and *no authority*." "The *authority* of Isaiah"—and all other inspired poets—" is quite sufficient." The authority of the Bible overrides all other authority : "supreme judicatory" to the contrary, notwithstanding. Has the author before us written "*common sense?*" himself being judge. P. 140.

SECONDLY.—OUR AUTHOR PLANS DIVINE INSPIRATION AND POETICAL GENIUS IN THE SAME CATEGORY.

One would think, at the very first glance, that to place in the same category, *Divine inspiration*, a supernatural gift of the Holy Spirit, and *poetical genius*, a merely natural and ordinary gift, is blunder enough in the commencement of a course of argument to condemn the whole process, without any reference to the conclusion. But this is the very thing we have for argument in the quotation before us. This is the very assumption of the premises on which the logical argument is built. "Individuals *may* employ their noble *poetical talents*, in composing hymns, as Luke employed his gift of inspiration in composing Acts iv. 24."

Now, we admit, "individuals *may* employ their noble poetical talents," in composing as many gospel sonnets as they please; but this "*may*"—this *if they please*, utterly fails to be like Luke's position. Look at it. Luke inspired, "*may*" write Acts iv. 24. Luke "*may employ*" his gift of inspiration in composing and writing down, as moved by the Spirit, Acts iv. 24. Luke *might* have chosen *not to employ his gift,* not to exercise his Christian privilege, *just as* many gifted Christian poets, free to exercise their Christian liberty, yet choose not to do so! "Poets, endowed by the 'Author of every good and perfect gift,' *may*, in composing hymns, gather from the Psalms, and from other portions of the sacred records, agreeably to the example of Luke, who gathered and composed, in the employment of his good and perfect gift of inspiration, a song from Ps. ii. and from other portions of the sacred records." Luke, by inspiration, gathering from many portions of the Bible, composed a song of praise, which the church might sing in her public worship, so soon as her supreme judicatory should issue her sanction! Had Luke chosen *not* to exercise his Christian privilege, *not* to employ his gift of inspiration in gathering the material and composing that excellent Psalm, Acts iv. 24; or had the supreme judicatory withheld her sanction, neither Peter, John, their company, nor Luke the writer, nor the church, could have enjoyed the privilege of singing in the public worship of God, that beautiful Psalm. For, "Agreeably to the example in Acts iv. 24, the poet *may* compose, by his poetical gift, hymns; and so soon as the supreme judicatory of the church shall issue her sanction, they may be sung by the worshipping people of God, but not till then. And this, remember, is the very thing involved in the issue—the gifted Christian poet, by poetic genius, may do what Luke did, by inspiration. Such is the assumption. Such is the conclusion. Like the tyro, closing his black-board demonstration, the author of this argument may, with self-complacency, exclaim—" *Quod demonstrandum erat!"* All this, however, is but to degrade divine inspiration, and to exalt ordinary poetic talent above its grade, to the disparagement of the extraordinary gifts of the Holy Spirit; and so dishonor God.

Thirdly.—Our author *denies* that the Head of the church inspired, qualified and appointed, even to compose, gather and arrange songs of praise for the use of the church— that such men did that work for the church by divine authority—that we have that work in the Bible as the prepared praise for the use of the church—as also, that any uninspired man may prepare songs of praise for the use of the church. On the other hand, he *affirms* that the preparing authority is in the church, represented by her supreme judicatory—that to sing a literal scripture psalm is "a mere modern invention, an innovation upon both inspired and uninspired authority." That THERE IS NOT A SOLITARY INSTANCE IN THE NEW TESTAMENT, OF THE SINGING OF A PSALM OF DAVID IN A "LITERAL" FORM. P. 80, etc. That "such sublime and beautiful portions of the sacred records—as Isa. xii. —are songs of praise *already made*, and whether they be found in the New or Old Testament, they are admirably suited to the worship of God. It would be easy to collect twice the number of the Psalms, of such admirable compositions." P. 140. Then follows a whole page of argument to establish the affirmation that it is lawful, and that we have *authority* from the word of God, to use this large collection of Bible songs, twice the number of the Psalms, in praising God.

The labyrinth of words, employed throughout this model work before us, of which we have here given but a specimen in the denials and affirmations, the assumptions and contradictions just noticed, suggests many curious inquiries. We offer a very brief specimen of many that might very justly be made, all of which require solution, to make the way of truth plain.

Had David any authority, by inspiration, to prepare songs of praise, for the use of the church? Or, did he—like Christian poets now—only "employ his noble poetical talents with which the Author of every good and perfect gift endowed him? And then, were the productions of his poetic genius subjected to the sanctioning authority of the Sanhedrim before they were 'prepared for the use of the church?' How was it? Had Isaiah, Asaph, Ezra, or any other poet or scribe of the law, any authority from the head of the church to compose, gather or arrange their own songs or the songs of others for the use of the church? Did Miriam, and David, and Isaiah, and Ezra—did any or all of those who composed, by divine inspiration, these songs of praise recorded in the Bible, 'twice the number of the Psalms,' sing their songs and Psalms in the worship of God, and the church with them, sing as we have them in the Bible, as the inspired word of God? Or, were these inspired songs sung in some other uninspired, unliteral form, than as transmitted to us, and so in the form sung, lost to us? Was it proper for them to sing those songs 'in a literal form,' since it is improper for us so to sing them? How are these things? Would it to them have been 'a mere modern invention and innovation, to have sung those songs in a literal form,' as 'made' and 'prepared' by those inspired writers?" Again:—

Had Luke, or Peter, or John, or their company, authority to compose and sing Acts iv. 24–30, as we have it recorded "in literal form"? Or, did they so sing it without its having been submitted to a Synod of apostles and elders? And then, have we those seven verses of that beautiful song, in Acts recorded, as composed by the poet, inspired or uninspired; or, have we it as examined and sanctioned by the apostolic college? And still farther—can we sing it as we find it in its "literal form," as Peter, and John, and their company sang it; or, must we have it "altered and adapted to *our* circumstances," and then examined, amended, and sanctioned by the supreme judicatory before it can be "prepared" for the use of the church, and sung in her public worship?

Did the author, in writing pp. 140, 141, forget what he had written—pp. 80 and 132, 133? In 80, he argues that the Psalms were never sung in a "literal form," in New Testament times—that the divine pattern for *making* New Testament Psalms is, by grouping as—"*just as* Dr. Watts and Presbyterians do," and as Peter, etc., did, Acts iv. 24 —that for this way of *making* psalms for the use of the church there is "express 'Divine appointment.'" In pp. 132, 133, he argues that poets may make and sing psalms as preachers may make and preach sermons—that any poet may compose, the supreme judicatory prepare and sanction, and the church sing the same—that this is the Presbyterian way. Yet, in p. 140, he says: "It is a plain dictate of common sense, that to versify such passages of the other scriptures, as Isa. xii., is no more "to make songs of praise than to versify the one hundred and fifty Psalms after the manner of Rouse. Such sublime and beautiful portions of the sacred records are songs of praise *already made*"—and whether in New or Old Testament are suitable to praise, and divinely authorized to be sung. "The *authority* of Isaiah is quite sufficient, if there were no other." Now, we may ask:

So far as *authority* to compose, prepare, or sanction is concerned, which is the authorized way—the Presbyterian way, or the way of Isaiah, pp. 140, 141? Or, had they one way under the Old Testament, viz.: singing in the "literal form" songs "already made," and another in the New Testament, "*just as* Dr. Watts and Presbyterians do"; and just as they say Peter, in Acts iv. 24, did? How are all these?

Again—In regard to the "multitude of the disciples" who sang part of Psalm cxviii—Luke xix. 38—"but with alterations adapted to the circumstances," what gifted poet, or which of the disciples, altered the Psalm, "just as Dr. Watts and Presbyterians do"? Or, did they all *impromptu* alter in unison and sing as it came from the poet, whoever that may have been? Or, did they sing it as sanctioned by the highest judicatory to which they were subordinate? How, and by what process, did "the whole multitude of the disciples," on the highway, in that grand procession, alter and adapt to circumstances, that Psalm, as Watts and Presbyterians do, securing the sanction of "supreme judicatory"? For, we suppose the loving disciples, right under the eye of the beloved Saviour, would not dare an "*invention* and *innovation*" by singing a "Psalm of David in a literal form"! Nor would the poetic multitude dare sing their own composition without the sanction of the church in the Presbyterian way! Or, after all, were the "multitude of the disciples," now escorting Christ in his triumphal entrance into Jerusalem, really holding prayer-meeting, for which they needed to prepare a Psalm "adapted to the circumstances"? Were they attending public worship and the preaching of the word by their Master, or some other preacher, and at the beginning of the service, or at its close, or both, had they—poor multitude, without Bible or Hymnal, really just then and there—to make a model hymn, and in a *model way*, "just as Dr. Watts and Presbyterians do"? "This *is* an inspired pattern for making New Testament Psalms"! Just in the likeness of this pattern, did any Christian poet, or any Christian church in the world, ever think or dream of making New Testament Psalms for the use of her public praise? Not in one single feature of this narrative has any church ever attempted to copy in preparing her songs. That the promiscuous crowd may have shouted their hosannas, and huzzas in the language of the Psalm; or, that they may have sung in unison words memorized, may, as a hypothesis, have some claim to common sense; but that in that triumphal march, in the shouting of the multitude, we can find a pattern for altering and modelling Bible Psalms, and making New Testament songs, is germain to the cause for which it is used.

And farther: We have "the song of Mary the mother of our Lord, and of Zacharias and Elizabeth, the song of the angels at the birth of Christ, and the numerous sublime hymns of praise in the Revelation." These examples of our author are songs and hymns, original compositions, and not Psalms, by "alteration, adapted to the circumstances." These are not examples of "grouping together the Psalms along with *other inspired matter, just* as Dr. Watts and Presbyterians do," for inspired matter grouped with other inspired matter would be inspired matter still; still the word of God; scripture, not merely scriptural. To the inquiring reader some curious inquiries are very naturally suggested here:

Did Mary, and Zacharias, and Elizabeth, and the angels, compose and write down their songs, as Watts and other gifted poets do? And Luke finding them, did he write them down in his history as he found their manuscripts? Or, was Luke inspired to record so much of what each of these persons "said" in mere extempore prayer, or thanksgiving in ejaculatory form, as the Spirit of inspiration directed him? If Mary and the angels, as gifted poets, composed and wrote their songs, did they submit them for the revision and sanction of the church, that they might be used in her public praise? Or, if their songs were inspired, then, whether they or Luke penned them, they are *scripture* psalms; and should they still be recomposed and made uninspired, as the hymnals are, and then subjected to supreme judicatory, before, by authority, they can be prepared and sung? And where shall we find the requisite amending and preparing judicatory to fit angel's songs, or inspired songs, for Presbyterian praise?

Now, in all this assumption of "inspired pattern for making" songs of praise for the use of the church, where, in all these cases of example, so boldly paraded, is there one single parallel line or point? If the Head of the church, by inspiring holy men; if, by his Spirit inditing to them songs of praise; if, by giving to his church, through those inspired men, inspired songs of praise perfectly adapted to that end, did not prepare and authorize for the use of the church in her public praise, then there is no authority in the church, or among men, to prepare songs for such use. When any theory or assumption, carried out to its legitimate consequences and conclusions, becomes absurd, and indeed ridiculous, it is time to abandon it. But to adduce the example of the multitude, Luke xix. 28, in making songs of praise for the use of the church in the public worship of God, is simply ludicrous!

Fourthly.—We notice, in the references to our author, want of logical candor, prejudicial to truth and fact. He tells his readers that the Presbyterian Church sanctions uninspired hymns, just as the Scottish General Assembly sanctioned Rouse. It is not charging too much to say. that the author endeavors to make the impression that the uninspired hymns of his church, for which no one lays claim of inspiration, are just as much inspired as the Scottish version of the Psalms, received and used by its friends as a translation. It is too late to attempt, by chicanery, to divert the intelligent reader from the real issue on the question of Psalmody. Scripture or scriptural, inspired or uninspired, are the indexical or representative terms too well known in this controversy to be evaded by a mere *dixit*.

That the Church of Scotland, in adopting the version of the Book of Psalms, still used by the churches which profess to use a scripture psalmody, meant to be understood as doing just the same thing as the supreme judicatory did in authorizing the hymnal of the present day, is not sustained by the leading facts of their respective histories. The one was passing upon a metrical *version*, or translation, of one of the books of the inspired Bible, diligently comparing with the original Hebrew text. The other was passing upon a collection of poems, without any pretensions by anybody, either poets or supreme judicatory, to being a version of anything, far less of any book of the Bible.

The Waldensian Church had chanted the Psalter, time immemorial. So Dr. Revel, Professor of Theology in the Waldensian Seminary, said in the writer's hearing twenty years ago. The Huguenots of France used a version of the Book of Psalms. The churches of the Netherlands, as early as the days of William the Silent, according to Motley's History, used a Flemish version of the Psalter. The Geneva and Scottish churches used the Psalter, in some kind of a version, how good or how indifferent, we leave for another connection, in which the merits of respective translations may be noticed. In the early days of the Reformation, " chant the Psalter " was, to all the churches referred to, a familiar phrase. In the course of time the question of psalmody was raised among them—" chant the Psalter," or sing a metrical version. At the second Reformation—the times of the Westminster Assembly—the Church of Scotland, while reforming other things, endeavored to secure a better version of the Book of Psalms. Whether introducing metrical versions, and bringing into use measured singing, instead of simply chanting the Psalter, was a wise measure, may be a question. But that the Church of Scotland, during her long labors in amending the Psalms versified by Rouse, and in making new versions of a large portion of the book, entertained neither the idea of a paraphrase in the sense now generally understood, nor in the sense especially used by our friends on the other side here, needs no elaborate argument. Even yet Webster gives, for "paraphrasing," "explaining or *translating amply and freely.*" So, even interpret is used for translating one language into another; as when the missionary goes first to the heathen he uses an interpreter till he acquires a knowledge of the native language. Arguments based on mere verbal criticism, and of words, too, whose use, after the lapse of a few hundred years, has suffered change, are not always conclusive. Men of candor, in grave religious controversy, will deal sparingly in such craft.

Now, whether the Scottish Assembly succeeded, in every instance, in giving " *The Book of Psalms in metre; translated and diligently compared with the original text, and former translations; more plain,* smoother *and agreeable to the text than any heretofore;*" as was understood on all hands she professed to give; or, whether she failed in some of her translations, as all translators may do, has about the same affinity to the issue before us as the question whether the version of King James is a better book than the Koran. King James' translation has *many mistranslations;* yet it is *The Bible:* the recognized Word of God, and, after all, a better book than the Koran, or Hymnal either.

To test the merits of the Scottish version of the Book of Psalms, as a correct translation, by King James' translation, before the unlearned masses, is simply to play small tricks: so, to say the supreme judicatory of the Presbyterian Church examines, *amends*, sanctions her hymnals, "just as the Scottish General Assembly sanctioned Rouse." In the one case one Assembly had to deal with "a version," a translation, whose ultimate test was the Hebrew text; and if, when amended, it was found to be a *better* translation, and *better* and *smoother* poetry, it was then to be substituted for a former and *worse* translation. That was the question and subject before the Scottish Assembly about two hundred and twenty-five years ago. In the other case the other Assembly has to do with a collection of poems: unlike the Book of Psalms, or any other book of the inspired Bible: a collection without any *ecclesiastical status* or authority whatever, from either the church or from her Head; and the use of this she sanctions, and clothes for the very first time with its first ecclesiastical and sacred swaddling-cloth. To pass upon translations is one thing: the translation of a book of the Bible; to pass, as a mere "Publication Board," or "Committee," upon any composition of man, is another thing. All this tilting with the terms "paraphrase" and "patchwork," in a question on the exclusive use of inspired songs in the worship of God, may be what its authors desire it to be, and so answer their end; one thing it cannot be: it cannot be an intelligent argument addressed to the understanding of an intelligent Christian who believes the Bible songs to be superior to all uninspired compositions, and who believes them to be given by the Head of the church for her praise, and who can find, *nowhere*, authority for any other. And farther: such cannot convince intelligent Bible Psalm-singers, who read from opponents, thus: "Where has God authorized any *uninspired man* to prepare songs of praise for the church? Presbyterians answer, *nowhere!*" And then, when they read the *assumption* without shadow of proof—the *popish assumption*—that the Head of the church has lodged the praise making power in supreme judicatory of the Presbyterian Church. And then, again, in the third place, when they read from the same pen: "Such sublime and beautiful portions of the *sacred records*, and whether they be found in the New or Old Testament, they are admirably suited to the worship of God." "But is it lawful to use them in praising God? What says the Holy Ghost by the writers of many of those passages? Sing unto the Lord: sing unto the Lord a new song." [Isa. xlii. 10.] "We think the *authority* of Isaiah is quite sufficient if there were no other." Such are the very positive statements in the work before us.

Now, as to the *first* and *third* of the above positions of our author, all agree: no man uninspired has authority to prepare songs of praise for the church; the songs prepared by the Holy Spirit, recorded in the Bible, are prepared and *authorized* for the use of the church in her worship. The *second* is the assumption in dispute: the authority of the supreme judicatory to prepare and *authorize*. For the following reasons this assumption is *false, presumptuous* and *dangerous:*

1. There is not the *shadow* of a hint of any such authority lodged exclusively in *supreme judicatory:* not a whit more than in any *uninspired man*, of whom it is so promptly denied. The proof offered here in support of the assumption is an insult to the Head of the church. He has promised to be with the ministry in the preaching of the gospel, and in administering the seals of the new covenant.

This teaching power never comes into a church *judicatory*. The ruling power only: elders, lay and ministerial, with parity of power, sit here together for *judgment*: for the administration of law, not for legislation. Church *judicatories* may never dare do what Christ, the Lawgiver, has done for his house and kingdom. But, as the only Lawgiver, and Author of all institutions and ordinances and rites of worship in his own house, he has prepared, given and authorized, by *inspired men*, songs of praise. No other is authorized to do any such thing. In any government, can any person or combination of persons do what the law commissioned an officer to do by commission? Try it in levying and collecting taxes. Try it in regard to *any legal* and *official function*, and learn whether the majesty of government and law be not insulted.

2. The assumption leads *necessarily* to confusion, heresy, sectarianism and schism. By their fruits ye shall know them. True, this is not the only source of these evils. Alas! only one of many. Anomalous, indeed, that any sect should fail to enstamp one single distinctive feature upon its hymnology. And nearly as anomalous, perhaps far more so, should any one of them all fail to be deeply tainted with error. Take this one, of a hundred examples which have had, or now have, a place in the hymnology of one of the most evangelical of the churches of this land:

> "O, if my soul were formed for woe, how would I vent my sighs,
> Repentance should like rivers flow, from both my streaming eyes.
> 'Twas for my sins my dearest Lord hung on the accursed tree;
> And groaned away a dying life, for thee, my soul, for thee."

We have seen the intelligent Armenian clench both lips and teeth while the first line was being sung: because he believed God never *formed* any *soul for woe*. And how any Calvinist could sing these four lines with understanding and heart we know not. While it was in the book and sung, it must have been sung by good people in ignorance; for how otherwise could sincere Christians sing a Saviour dying for souls *formed for woe,* and such souls the subject of the Spirit's grace, *repentance?* Like this: how many hundred hymns, in singing which, would it not be better to listen to the organ, and attach no meaning whatever?

Take another example, and still worse, because it horribly mutilates and perverts a beautiful gospel portion of God's word to the cause of error. Not an example of expurgated composition, to whose glaring absurdity use and public sentiment have directed attention and final expurgation; but a par excellent, current song, exhibited as of specimen interest, the boast of representative advocates of a human psalmody: a pattern specimen of *the correct rendering* of the very words of divine inspiration, putting Rouse to the blush, and throwing the test standard itself, King James' Bible, in the shade.

Here is "the correct rendering" (!) of these words found in the first clause of the 10th verse of the xvith Psalm: "For thou wilt not leave my soul in hell." "Though in the dust I lay my head, yet, gracious God, thou wilt not leave my soul forever with the dead." With the *translation* we will deal in another connection. The heresy of this boasted pattern of human composition is now before us. Mark well this specimen of "the correct rendering" of the words of the Holy Spirit: this specimen of enchanting, beautiful "gospel turn," in turning David into a Christian, and Christ out of this Psalm, and the doctrine of the resurrection of his body mystified by the murky clouds of pagan limbo and popish purgatory for the *soul:* this specimen of deep, dishonoring, semi-infidel thrust at the Saviour, turning a blessed portion of his own word, testifying of himself, into a kind of parody upon David: this specimen of the necessity, from consistency, and the power of error, of throwing a thick vail over the Psalms to hide Christ from the view of faith and the worshipper, and so play into the hand of a human psalmody. Of this specimen of "the correct rendering," we charge:

1. As a pretended *rendering* of that portion of God's word, which has the *resurrection* of Christ's *body* for its subject, *it is sheer nonsense*. For, Christ had but *one* human *soul* and *one* human *body*. At his death, that *one soul* passed immediately into glory, where there is *no death*. His *one body* was laid in the *grave*, a *visible place*. He had no *third part* that could go *with the dead*, the limbo or *hades* of the *Pagan*, or the purgatory of the *Papist:* the *invisible* or *separate place of the dead*.

2. It is *sheer heresy*. Christ's soul—David's, or the Christian's, by Watts—was never, at any time, even while his body lay in the grave, *with the dead*, in any orthodox, or evangelical sense. In this line of the Psalm there is no reference to Christ's *soul;* not one word.

3. It is the heresy of *popish purgatory*. But what is that? Simply that limbo, that purgatory, where *departed souls* go, that *separate place*, neither heaven nor hell, nor yet the *grave*, where Christ's *body* was laid; that place, or no place, *with the dead*.

This idea, of the old English sense of the Hebrew *sheol* and the Greek *hades*, as applied by Dr. Watts to the line of the Psalm before us, is derived from dark pagandom, baptized by popery. The heathen writers, knowing nothing of the soul's future state, nothing of its immortality, wrote of death much like their disciples of the French infidel school. Death an eternal sleep. The dark future. The invisible world. The unknown state of the *soul* after death. With this state of the *soul*, the heathen associated the expressive word *hades*, whose very etymology settles its application, *unseen, invisible.* The Christian sees, with the eye of sense, where the *body* is laid. He sees, with an eye of faith, where the *soul* goes. A paganized church, only, needs a third place, *with the dead,* where Watts' *correct rendering* sends the *soul,* while he sings of the *body*: "Though in the dust I lay my head"—

But, then, it is beautiful poetry. And how many pious souls, with characteristic sneer looking down upon the Psalm-singers, can, in most heavenly raptures, sing this very nonsense and popish heresy. Is ignorance the mother of devotion? It must be so! for how can any Christian, with the understanding, sing this specimen? Could psalm-explaining set all right here? All the efforts of all the Doctors of Divinity in the world can make neither truth nor sense of it. Perhaps just here lies the secret charm of poetry: mystery wrapt in clouds and darkness, and imagination transported into the awful invisible!

We have neither time nor space to review all the sectarian hymn-books in use among the churches, from the most evangelical down to the Arian, the Universalist and the Roman Catholic societies. In the face of them all, one fact is beyond controversy—the songs of the Bible are perfect. On the other hand, all these sectarian hymn-books are full of sectarian heresy and contradiction. How can it be otherwise? Catholic hymns savor not of protestantism. Immersers will hardly fail to sing their darling distinctive—the efficacy of "much water." The Universalist will be slow to conceal from his hymnology his all-glorious, happy, helless future. And so through the whole labyrinth of sectarian hymnology from entrance to exit. The *assumption*, then, is false, presumptuous and dangerous, because,

3. Against such the Head of the church has made ample provision. We shall be content here with the concessions

of our friends. They concede *first*, that no *uninspired man* is authorized to prepare songs for the church. They concede *secondly*, that in the sacred records are sublime and beautiful songs of praise *already made*. They concede *thirdly*, that those songs are *admirably suited* to the worship of God, whether found in New or Old Testament. They concede *fourthly*, that God has *authorized* these to be used in his worship. They concede in the *fifth* place, "that it would be easy to collect *twice the number of the Psalms*, of such admirable composition, *authorized* by the Head of the church, to be used in his worship." There are some two thousand four hundred verses of praise in the Book of Psalms. "Twice the number added" will make over *seven thousand* verses of sacred song, without error, infallible, all *admirably suited* for God's worship. This collection would make a hymn-book, all scripture, of about twelve hundred pieces, of six verses each.

Now, in regard to this collection, and in view of the concessions referred to, some queries are suggested for the consideration of the friends of the unity of the body of Christ.

Would not such a collection, made with judgment, be satisfactory to all as to its largeness and its variety of matter? Would it not be orthodox?—orthodox enough for all evangelical Christians? Would it not be perfect?—perfect as other parts of God's word? Would it not all be suitable to the worship of God? Would it not be superior to every other hymn-book now in use in any of the churches? Might it not be a basis of union for all the evangelical churches, so far as psalmody is concerned? Would not the offer of such a hymnology, as a basis of union, give to the church offering it a vantage ground over all the other churches? And might it not be well to remember that there is no creed, or term of communion, with any evangelical church, making the use of such a collection a bar to fellowship?—"the compositions of uninspired men" only.

Fifthly.—In this quotation before us, we have an attempt to conceal fallacy, and use it for argument. While it concedes that there is neither authority, nor promise of aid, for any uninspired man to prepare psalms, for the use of the church; yet, by a little tact in transferring a promise from its designed and specified object to another, not contemplated at all, the end seems to be gained. "There are precious and abundant promises to the church of Christ, that the presence of the Holy Spirit shall be with her public councils." Here borrowing promised presence, and using it for the purpose of doing her own will, instead of her Master's—in preparing psalms for the use of the church, a work the Master has reserved for himself; a work to which He has neither appointed her councils, nor for which promised his Spirit. Again—"Has he not promised to be with her ' to the end of the world?' Here is borrowing promise and presence. *First,* from the gospel ministry, and giving to church councils. *Second,* from the work of preaching the gospel, to the work of 'preparing songs of praise for the church,' a work which 'no uninspired man' may do, as conceded. Might not our author as well borrow a little 'inspiration' for the occasion, or Peter's key to complete the infallibility ?"

True, Christ has commissioned and commanded the missionary of the cross, to go into all the world and preach —True, he has promised to go with the missionary in this work of preaching "to the end of the world;" but is it true that he has *commissioned* and *commanded* church councils to make psalms for the church, or that he has promised either his Spirit or presence in any such work? And has a "supreme judicatory" the right to assume the

Master's work, and then beg, or borrow promises to shield her in her bold assumption? Or, are divine commissions and promises convertible, so that any promise, made to any other one commissioned to any specified work, may be claimed by church councils, when they may please to assume any work to which they have not the shadow of a call? Christ has promised his presence to the dying saint while passing through the dark valley of the shadow of death; *therefore*, Christ has promised his presence to the public councils of the church in preparing psalms for her use! Christ has promised to go with the missionary to preach; *therefore*, he will be with "supreme judicatory," in making psalms! What else might she not do, just as Romish conclave does, under covert of the missionary's promise—"Lo, I am with you, to the end of the world?" "Thou art Peter, and upon this rock I will build my church!"

That we are not here mistaken in regard to the fallacious assumption, what closes the quotation, makes evident—"And have we not at least as good grounds to hope for this gracious presence with the collective 'body of Christ,' when the church is amending and authorizing these songs of praise, as when uninspired men of the United Presbyterian persuasion are *explaining* Rouse to their congregations, and putting into their hearts the sentiments which they shall feel when uttering the language of the paraphrase?"

A brief analysis of our author's argument here: 1. He *assumes* that the Scottish version of the Book of Psalms is no more scripture than Watts—nothing but Rouse's paraphrase—not scripture at all. 2. From this assumption he justly infers, that we have no right to use this version as we use the scriptures, making it a Text-Book from which to preach, just as Christ used the Book in which he found Isa. lxi. 1, 2, from which he lectured, or expounded, or preached as recorded in Luke iv. 18–22. 3. He then concludes, that his church council is about as safe, as to authority, and Christ's promised presence, in making and authorizing psalms for the use of the church, as we are in using in the pulpit, ministerially, a doggerel paraphrase for the Bible. That is, all this claim of council is as silly as the silly thing to which he compares it. While this may do very well as disparagement of the claim of authority and the Master's presence in the work of psalm-explaining, it destroys the high claims of councils for psalm-making.

But the assumption being false, the whole argument built upon it, is alike false. The Scottish version is scripture, if the Septuagint from which Christ and his Apostles quoted and preached is scripture. And it is too late to blot out the Septuagint from the long recognized list of translations of the Bible. And so, it is too late to cast off the Scottish version, a better one than the one recognized and used as scripture in Christ's and his Apostles' times. And yet, whenever our author, or his friends, with Hebrew Bible in hand, will show us that the Scottish version of the psalms is a worse translation than the Septuagint; so much worse, that it cannot be recognized as scripture, then will we consider that our ministerial expositions of our metrical translation of the Book of Psalms, are as trifling as church councils making psalms for the worship of God. Till this shall be done, United Presbyterian ministers, by virtue of their commission to expound the whole Word of God—as Christ from a translation—will continue, as ever, to expound the Book of Psalms, either in prose or poesy translation, or from the Hebrew text itself; for they explain sometimes from one, sometimes from another, sometimes availing themselves of all three, and oftentimes even of more.

In the *sixth place*.—This whole claim of church prerogative here assumed, is essentially popish. It all proceeds on the assumption of New Testament privilege—Christian liberty—liberty of "supreme judicatory," to establish anything in the worship of God she pleases, not expressly forbidden.

It has ever been the glory of Protestantism, in every protestant country, and among all the departments of the protestant family, not turned back toward popery, to contend for the simplicity and purity of the worship of God, as instituted in his word; and to protest against all ways of worship of mere human device—"any other way not appointed in the Word." The Catholic tells us he may worship God any way holy mother church ordains, if not forbidden; and therefore, because the worship of the sacramental wafer is not expressly among forbidden objects, and because the church by prerogative, decrees this Christian liberty, and enjoins its exercise upon her credulous children, the obedient son bows in homage reverently before the body, blood and presence of the Saviour! So, he can bow before the image of the "Mother of God," or the image of any of the saints canonized by church prerogative. Popery can make or unmake, objects and ways of worship, ordain and annul ceremonies and rites, bind and loose the conscience at will.

So, too, say some protestants, as the church of England in her claims of ritualistic privilege, and so in the claims of "supreme judicatory," to make and unmake matter and manual of praise, and bind the same upon the church. "For, there are precious and *abundant* promises to 'The church of Christ,' that the presence of the Holy Spirit shall be with her *public councils*—with the collective 'body of Christ,' when the church is amending and authorizing these songs of praise:" these songs of praise composed without authority by uninspired men, but to be used in the worship of God by authority of church council. By the very same assumed authority in council, Rome authorizes Mass. By the very same authority in council, the church of England authorizes her Prayer-Book, and all the mummery of her empty, vain ceremonies. By this same authority in councils of the church, presumptuously claimed, all the abominations of the mother of harlots, all the trumpery of ritualism have been introduced and sustained from the days of Constantine till now. No one claims Bible authority for either Mass, or Prayer-Book, or Hymnal. All sustained upon the same pious (!) plea for pictures, crosses, images—all to quicken and aid devotion in the worship of God—and their institution at the will of church council. "The end sanctifies the means;" and the council determines what means will promote the end.

But then, we are told that this is all done "*just as* the Scottish General Assembly sanctioned Rouse." Now we have seen that the Assembly, passing upon the Scottish version, passed upon a translation, comparing, at every step, "with the Hebrew text, *and* former translations." Such is never thought of in the other cases. Watts was too good a man, and too honest, to permit it to go to the world, that either his imitations or hymns were to be tested in their adoption by church council, by original text, Hebrew or Greek.

That the church, whose business it is to see that the law shall go forth of Zion, and the word of the Lord from Jerusalem, to every people, language, and tongue, may supervise translations of the Bible, and authorize them as safe translations for her missionaries to carry to the heathen, whether in prose or poetry, to be read or sung, is a matter about which there can be no dispute, and about which the question of the right of councils to authorize the manner and matter of worship can have as little concern. This preparing and sending abroad the Bible in so many translations is a matter bearing very little analogy, and certainly no parallelism, to the authorizing of written prayers or uninspired hymns for the use of the church in worship. But it is like the church preparing a metrical *translation* of the Book of Psalms for the use of her assemblies worshipping in any other than the Hebrew language. It is analogous to the church's examining King James' translation, and authorizing it *as such*, to be used in families and churches. It is like authority competent, deciding upon translations of the Bible, whether that authority be *parental* for the family, *ecclesiastical* for the church, *civil* for the state; or whether in all, or none of them, is a matter of little concern in this discussion. Wherever the authority lies, or whoever may exercise it, this is certain: it involves no such right as the making of a new Bible in whole or in part, for any purpose for which God made and gave the Bible. God prepared and gave the whole Bible to be read, studied, believed, and obeyed. Some parts of the Bible He prepared to be sung, gave to be sung, "*authorized* to be sung to his praise in worship." Has the translating of the Bible, and the authorizing the use of that translation of the Bible, as the word of God, anything to do with the question of divinely appointed worship, all of which has its appointment there; or, with the right of all to use that Bible, translated, or untranslated, if they can acquire a competent knowledge of the original text? Is the composing of hymns a parallel to the translating of the Bible, or any part of it, into the English language, prose or poetry? If Christ and his apostles used a translation of the Bible as the word of

God, then, may not the church send the Bible to the heathen translated into all their languages, without involving the authority of making a prayer-book and hymn-book for them, as if all proceeded upon the same principle? Rome assumes that the scriptures are not to be read, or used by the people, till authorized by the highest power in the church. Families, prayer-meetings, congregations, may not use them without church authority. Poets may scribble poems, but families, prayer-meetings, and congregations may not sing them till authorized by "supreme judicatory"; then it is the right of all to worship God with the hymns authorized by church council. This is the assumption: the right to worship, not as God has appointed in his word, but as high church prerogative authorizes. This is popish.—Because every man, antecedent to any church authority, interposed, has from God the Bible addressed and given to himself, free to use by direct authority from God, the Author, for every purpose for which He prepared and gave it, and in every capacity and relation in which it is needed, and for which it is "suited" —to read it, search it, *sing* it in God's praise, worshipping with it in the use of its God-given songs. Every family, antecedently to, and independently of, any *pope*, or "supreme judicatory," may use, read, and sing, and with it praise God in his worship. So of man, individually or socially, in all acts of worship. And more; man, in all these conditions and relations, having the Bible, may by it test the sermons of the ministry, by it test every act and authorization of *every judicatory*, supreme and subordinate, by original right from God derived—a right with which neither *pope* nor "supreme judicatory" can interfere.

Now, this is the sum of the issue here: God's Bible commands all, individually and socially, to praise him.

The family, the prayer-meeting, the congregation assembled, are commanded to sing praise. And for every family God has given the Bible to be used for all purposes for which he gave it; to be read and to be *sung* in the worship of God at the family altar. So, to every prayer-meeting He has given the Bible to be used for the same purposes, in the social worship. And in like manner to every worshipping congregation for similar uses. Then, every family, prayer-meeting, congregation, is furnished by the Head of the church with "suitable" *songs* to be *sung*, with "authority" to *sing* them and with ample directions *how* they must be *sung*. Where comes in the church authority to interfere with any use of the Bible for which God authorized it? Suppose the Pope and "supreme judicatory" had never authorized either the reading or singing of the Bible, and should never do so; what, in all that, detrimental to the perfect right of the people and of the church to worship God, to pray, or *praise*, or read his word? True, no man may go forth and preach this Bible, given to all, to be read, and searched, and *sung* by all, till authorized by the laying on of the hands of the Presbytery: then he may go and preach it. Then he may go to any gathering of the people, and to them expound that Bible in the name and by the authority of the Head of the church, whose ambassador he is; but he is not obliged to carry with him written sermons, or prayer-books, or *hymnals*, prepared and authorized by either pope or council. He may go, carrying with him nothing from the church but the formal certificate, for order's sake, from the ordaining Presbytery, of his appointment by Christ to preach. He may carry his Bible, received from God's hand, and preach from it, and read it, and *sing* it with the worshipping people to whom he ministers, and so conduct, and perform, and *exemplify* all God's institutions of public worship, as really and perfectly without any other papal or church authority enforcing ritual, prayer-book, service or hymnal; and better than if supplemented and burdened with them all.

Suppose, again, that the "supreme judicatory" should, on review of her authorized hymns, discover they were unscriptural, or otherwise unpalatable, or unfashionable, and withdraw her authorization, and tell the people and the poet that they are unauthorized, and not to be sung; and yet, the poet who penned them, and the people who had been accustomed to sing them in worship, would choose to sing them still—what then? Would it be wrong to sing them? Don't the different sects reciprocally sing each other's hymns, with or without authority of "supreme judicatory"? Or, should "supreme judicatory" please to re-enact her rejected hymns, would that make it right again to sing them? Is there any *right* or *wrong* in the matter to infringe a tranquil conscience? Can the "supreme judicatory" make the same thing right or wrong at pleasure?

But further, here: Had the "supreme judicatory" never passed upon the said hymns at all, must it have been wrong for the gifted poet, and the people for whom God gifted him, to use them in the worship of God? And had neither "unauthorized" poet nor authorizing "judicatory" moved in the matter at all, and should they never, what then? Would the people of God, the whole church, the whole world, have remained, and through all time still remain, without matter of social praise authorized to be sung in the worship of God? And must God have remained unworshipped and unsung in psalms, and hymns, and spiritual songs? Would not the whole Bible furnish, by authority unquestioned, material enough for social chanting of God's praise, had he never given a gifted poet, uninspired, to the church, or an edict of a supreme judicatory?—For he has promised neither, nor is either among the gifts received by our ascended Lord, through which to endow his church with matter of praise. This claim of "supreme judicatory" to prepare and authorize praise for the use of the church is essentially usurped and popish.

CHAPTER IV.

EXAMINATION OF SCRIPTURE AUTHORITY CLAIMED FOR MAKING AND USING, IN THE FORMAL WORSHIP OF GOD, UNINSPIRED SONGS.

In what we agree—In what we differ—Demand of negative proof unreasonable—In the true issue our brethren affirm—Five affirmative Proof-Texts for the Presbyterian system of Psalmody—Our friends argue both sides of the true issue—Irrelevant verbal criticism—Appeal to reason and argument from the "stronghold" texts—Authority from command—A representative paragraph examined—The leading point of assumption, its identities and deductions therefrom—The argument from scripture example—Entrance into Jerusalem, Luke xix. 38—"Pattern" for Presbyterian hymn-making—The second "pattern" case for so making, Acts iv. 24—Impromptu Prayer-meeting, or Committee on Revision of Bible Psalms—Commentators—Barnes and Jacobus—Reflections.

IN examining the foundation on which our friends lay their claims of right to make their own psalms, hymns, and songs of praise, in the worship of God, we invite attention to a few preliminaries. In all successful discussion, having union in view, it will be well to know wherein we agree, and where we differ. It may be well to know, also, if anything can be compromised, and what.

We all agree that we may make our own sermons, and preach them, without any inspiration. We all agree that we may, by the promised inditing of the Spirit, as peculiar to prayer, make our own impromptu prayers; the veritable desires of the heart, without pen, or book, or manual. We all agree that singing with the voice, from the Book, many in unison, and with the understanding and heart, is an ordinance of religious worship, appointed in the word of God. We all agree that "the only acceptable way of worshipping the true God is instituted by himself, and so limited by his own revealed will, that he may not be worshipped according to the imaginations and devices of men, or any other way not appointed in his word." We all agree that the *songs* of the Bible, divinely inspired, not only may be sung in the worship of God, but that God prepared them, gave them, and "authorized" them to be sung. Thus far we may as well refrain from controversy.

True, on one hand, the practice has been confined to the Book of Psalms, while, in principle, uncompromised in regard to the use of other inspired songs, suitable for praise. It is a remarkable feature of the providence of the Head of the church that has led all the psalm-singing churches to leave, in their organic law, the question of the use of "other scripture songs" an open one—one subject to interpretation, or application, as circumstances may suggest.

One thing, however, we cannot ignore. We disclaim all authority and right to make and use uninspired songs of praise in the formal worship of God. Here we stand still, and feel that we cannot proceed beyond the use of the inspired songs of the Bible in the worship of God, till our brethren show us the Divine way clearly marked. Here they diverge from the way, or advance and leave us, under the assumed authority and right of making, authorizing, and using in worship, songs uninspired—songs that will incorporate, in their own way of stating them, the essential doctrines of the Bible, so as to operate as a test of orthodoxy, as far as in their judgments essentials are concerned.

Our brethren seem confidently assured they have a divine warrant for composing and singing uninspired songs in worship. We as confidently believe they have not.

They affirm. We deny. They proceed. We stand still. They affirm the way is open. And, for reasons, they invite us to follow. We hear and weigh their reasons. We do not ask them to prove negatives. We are unwilling they should ask us to prove what neither they nor we deny—authority to sing Bible songs.

And since our brethren affirm, and offer the evidence on which rests the assertion of their right to make their own denominational Presbyterian Hymnal, it is certainly our privilege to cross-examine their evidence in chief. Nor will it be conceded here that the order of all honorable discussion shall be reversed by demanding of us "A divine warrant for *restricting* the praise of the church to inspired composition." You admit we have authority thus far. And more: You have affirmed with us, over and over again, this same authority. We then beg leave to be excused from undertaking any such absurd task as to prove here what nobody denies. But we are determined to hold you to your affirmation of your authority to go beyond our common ground, and use your own *homemade* matter of praise. Nor shall we be diverted by the common-place chicanery of your trained controversialists, as the following specimen exemplifies:

"It is true, indeed, that those texts (Col. iii. 16; Eph. v. 19,) have always been viewed as strongholds of the Presbyterian doctrine, viz.: that it is the duty and privilege of the church to praise God, not only with *Psalms*, but with any other hymns and songs found in the *inspired writings* (!) But our brethren have endeavored to turn this old Presbyterian battery against us."

Is this not a specimen of "unfair artifice, to perplex a cause, and obscure the truth"? Does this state either the principle or practice of the Presbyterian Church? Don't they plead the right of the Presbyterian Church, in her "supreme judicatory," to take up the poems of Watts, of Tom Moore, of Walter Scott, of Hannah Moore, of Mrs. Hemans, of Mrs. Sigourney—examine, sanction, and sing them to the praise of God in his worship? And are these, and their like, "inspired writings"? Inspired writings! Tom Moore inspired—or supreme judicatory! Which? What can our brethren mean when they foist inspiration into the controversy in such connection?

Our brethren have another side, for we are gravely told that

"The principles on which the Presbyterian system of psalmody is formed, are substantially the same as those on which all exposition, especially all lecturing upon select passages of scripture, is conducted; the principles on which ministers compose their prayers, and *explain the Psalms;* the principles on which the church assumes the immense responsibility of constructing her creed and catechisms; in a word, the same principles by which the church, as all admit, assumes the control and direction, under responsibility to God, *of every other part* of Divine worship."

In controversy, as in medical practice, alterations are sometimes, from patients' tastes, found expedient. Another specimen of the first side of the Presbyterian principles, here. Again, they say:

"The inspired pattern for making New Testament Psalms is, to group together parts of the Psalms, along with other inspired matter, just as Dr. Watts and Presbyterians do."

Now, after all this profession of "the Presbyterian system of psalmody"—"the duty and privilege of the church to praise God, not only with *Psalms*, but with other hymns and songs found in the inspired writings"—"grouping together different parts of God's word," still, the Presbyterian way is, that the "gifted poet may employ his noble poetical talents," as Watts, by converting David, or even Horace, into a Christian, as the inspiration of the *muse* should happen to lead; no matter who, what, or how, if sanctioned by standing committee, or "supreme judicatory," the composition has the Divine appointment to be employed in the worship of God. " The church assumes the immense responsibility," and to the word of God we are referred for authority in the assumption of such *high church prerogative.*

FIVE TEXTS OF SCRIPTURE CLAIMED AS AUTHORITY FOR THE PRESBYTERIAN SYSTEM OF PSALMODY.

These are the Texts, in the order in which they are used in the argument:—

"How is it then, brethren? when ye come together, every one of you hath a psalm." 1 Cor. xiv. 26.

"Speaking to yourselves in psalms and hymns, and spiritual songs." Eph. v. 19. "Let the word of Christ dwell in you richly in all wisdom; teaching and admonishing one another in psalms and hymns, and spiritual songs, singing with grace in your hearts to the Lord." Col. iii. 16. On these, our brethren rest the argument for *Divine authority*, for making and using uninspired songs, in the worship of God. The following are used as *inspired pattern for making New Testament Psalms:*

"Saying, "Blessed be the King that cometh in the name of the Lord; peace in heaven, and glory in the highest." Luke xix. 38. "And when they heard that, they lifted up their voice to God with one accord, and said, Lord thou art God, which hast made heaven and earth, and the sea, and all that in them is." Acts iv. 24.

It will be well here to fix in our minds, definitely, the subject under controversy; the very thing affirmed, and to be proved by the "stronghold" texts, to which we are referred as establishing "the Presbyterian doctrine." This is the affirmation—the church has authority to receive uninspired songs, composed by the poets, and to prepare them as stated in these words—"She examines, and where found needful, *amends* these productions, and then issues her sanction to their adoption in public worship."

Our friends here, in adjusting their stand point, from which to defend their stronghold, and manage their aggressive controversy in the use of their affirmative evidence, in the cause of their Divine right of uninspired praise, show how convenient it is to argue both sides, when in the wrong in controversy. They begin with an array of commentaries to settle the meaning of their leading text. These, too, are all of the hymn singing class, among which we have Dr. Hodge's, which says:—

"In 1 Cor. xiv. 26, where *psalmon* appears to mean such a *song given by inspiration*, and not one of the Psalms of David." "Such," adds a champion author, "is the unanimous testimony of these commentators." What do these commentators' friends of uninspired hymns mean, in giving this interpretation of this "stronghold" text? Do they mean that all these psalms, hymns and songs of the New Testament are, indeed, "given by inspiration?" Certainly, there is no need of such affirmative testimony here. All admit their inspiration. And then, what can this prove? Does it prove the Divine right of Presbyterian supreme judicatories to *make* and authorize the use of *uninspired* songs, the very matter of the affirmation in this controversy? If Paul, by inspiration, designed to teach us our privilege and our duty to sing other inspired songs, in addition to the Book of Psalms—and this seems to be the sum of all the commentaries, and arguments drawn from this source—is it not rather negative testimony against uninspired hymns and songs? If commanded to sing Bible songs, that seems to hint, at least, that we are not authorized to sing beyond the songs specified. If God specifically requires a lamb for sacrifice, and since no sacrifice can be accepted without specific appointment, by what legerdemain is a pig authorized? Ah, we are just here told, "where there is no law, there is no transgression;" and there is no law "restricting" to the lamb! So holy mother demands proof, affirmatively, for "restricting" to bread and wine in the Supper, and for our want of affirmative proof in a negative issue, she asserts her right to the wafer, and cries, when forbidden? So, our brethren, explaining their proof-texts, tell us the psalms in question, which Paul commanded to be sung, were certainly *inspired;* but infer from the command their authority to *make* and *sing* their own *uninspired* songs. May not the envelope here, like Benjamin's sack, wrap up too much? Joseph's cup was not Benjamin's corn.

To prepare the way for the best possible use of their "stronghold" proof texts, a large amount of philological skill, in very common-place, verbal criticism, has been expended by our friends, in making plain things dark and doubtful. Every available confusion has been thrown around the meaning of "Psalms, hymns and spiritual songs." And the confusion of the Septuagint is added to make confusion more confused. After the *endurance* of mountain labor, under the pressure of the *Hebrew Titles*, *Mizmorim*, *Tehillim*, *Shirim*, and the corresponding Greek, *Psalmais*, *humnais*, *odais*—added to these *Tehillah*, the singular of *Tehillim*—then *humnas* and *ainesis*, are yet added, *Negineth*, translated *humnais, hymns*, still more, *odais pneumatikais*, and *ode* not a *spiritual song!* And what! some four or five pages *delivered!* After reading the last page, we are as wise as we were before we waded through this labyrinth of words.

Well, we do learn that the Septuagint uses different words for the same thing, as *Asma* and *Oide* for the Hebrew *Shir;* and also, that its use of words is not very reliable, though it has long held an acknowledged place among translations of the Bible. Another thing we learn by this very circuitous criticism, we are just where we were at the beginning of the chapter. The Psalms in question are proved to be veritable *inspired writings.* The sum of the painful research is given in these words:—

"The two last terms, *humnas* and *ode*, are used by the Septuagint to designate other portions of the *inspired writings;* and why may not Paul have referred to those other *hymns* and *songs* not embraced in the Book of Psalms?" Referring to the inspired songs in Isa. xlii. 10; Deut. xxxi. 19, and Deut. xxxii., it is added: "Why may not the Apostle have had his eye upon such *humnai* and *odai*, 'hymns and songs,' as these, as they are found outside of the Book of Psalms? If he had reference to such as these, then what becomes of the argument of these brethren? Paul's exhortation to sing 'hymns and spiritual songs' becomes an inspired authority for the Presbyterian doctrine of psalmody."

Now, it is pretty evident, even to a tyro, that our friends here do pretty clearly prove something. But what? This is the question. Let us see. Do they not prove, or evidently labor to prove these:—

1. There are, in the Bible, *inspired writings,* called and designated *Psalms, hymns and spiritual songs.*

2. That the Apostle Paul, in the *proof-texts* before us, did mean these veritable *inspired writings,* in his exhortations to sing Psalms, hymns and spiritual songs.

3. That this is Divine authority, for singing the inspired songs of the Bible.

These truisms, denied by no church in the world, so far as we know, do not satisfy our friends; but with a *coup de grace*, most gracefully, indeed, they close by adding: *Becomes an inspired authority for the Presbyterian doctrine of psalmody!* That is—for our Presbyterian brethren, when arguing this question of psalmody, certainly believe their own logic— "the Presbyterian doctrine of psalmody," is to sing the *inspired writings,* the songs of the Bible! Do they wish us to believe this logic? Paul commands to *sing* inspired Bible songs; therefore he authorizes Presbyterians to *make* and *sing* Presbyterian hymns, which they, and everybody else, know are not the Psalms, etc., designated by the apostles.

If anything is proved by this labored appeal to verbal criticism, it is this simply, and nothing more: The apostle refers, not exclusively to the Book of Psalms, but to "other *inspired songs* of the Bible" as well. There is not even an attempt to prove more.

APPEAL TO REASON AND ARGUMENT FROM THE "STRONGHOLD" TEXTS.

Bear with us in quoting a paragraph, embracing the whole argument, drawn from the first three texts, in the order referred to, for authority to *make* and *sing uninspired* hymns.

"But it is replied that the churches of Ephesus and Colosse had in their possession the Psalms of David, and no other, therefore they would most certainly understand the Apostle as referring to the Book of Psalms alone."

On this sentence, as we pass, we remark, 1. It is not true that we assert, those churches had David's Psalms, and had no other. 2. It is not true that we assert, that these churches certainly understood the apostle as speaking of the "Book of Psalms *alone*." These churches had the whole Old Testament, and may have understood the apostle as speaking of all the Psalms of the Bible, so far as then known to compose the psalmody of all the churches. It is farther affirmed:

"But it seems to be forgotten that those churches were recently formed, amid a heathen population, and in heathen cities: books were scarce, and having to be copied by the hand on wax, lead, parchment or similar materials, were extremely expensive; and the ability to read was by no means general."

In regard to the import of this sentence, we ask the reader to notice,

1. The design of the statement, as in aid of the cause of uninspired hymns. This is the object they have for its statements.

2. These churches were formed amid illiterate brethren; they had few books; few were able to read the books they had; therefore, they could know little, if anything, of the Book of Psalms; little of what the Jews sung in their worship.

3. They had, nevertheless, extensive knowledge of uninspired hymns, made by Christians, the "membership" of these churches, so much and so general that all would at once understand Paul as referring to Presbyterian hymns, made in the Presbyterian way: by poet and "supreme judicatory."

4. Especially, notice, *how could* they know so *little* of Bible Psalms, and so *much* of uninspired hymns? Does the Bible, reason, or common sense, or history, or anything else make clear? *How?*

5. A question here: Do our brethren mean to ignore

the fact that wherever Paul went, throughout Eastern Europe or Western Asia, he found synagogues, and in them the Bible? To ignore the fact that everywhere among the Jews, of those regions, the Septuagint, in the vernacular tongue, that in which the New Testament was written, the language in which these very epistles were written, was in use, and had been for about three hundred years? Indeed? Have we Psalm-singers "forgotten" that Paul's converts and organized churches were so ignorant of the Bible, while all were so intimately acquainted with the hymn-book? Let us not forget this. It is so essential to an understanding of the argument here drawn from these *stronghold* texts. Of course, we *should not forget* that Paul's converts and churches must have been like our hymn-singing churches now, better acquainted with their hymn-books than their Bibles! To such state of things, or to such Christians as described, our brethren's theory will be very agreeable. Perhaps they understand the temper of their readers. What a beautiful sight! See those Christians wending their way to church; each a hymn-book under the arm; in the pew not a Bible. "Ability to read was by no means general." Of course *they* understood Paul. We would not forget, dear brethren; we have not "forgotten" the tendency of hymn-singing. We hope you will not forget.

But our friends have a compensation for the want of books, and the want of "ability to read" them. The main thing in the paragraph here follows—the pivotal point on which their argument turns.

"Besides; when the apostle rebukes the Corinthians as follows, 'Every one of you hath a Psalm'—the common interpretation is, that these *Psalms* were the fruits of the gifts of the Holy Spirit, then bestowed on the membership of the Corinthian church. Then, why might not the same divine influence have been found at Ephesus and Colosse? And why may not Paul refer to this class of Psalms, as well as to those of David? In view of the whole argument, it appears *most evident*, as Dr. Hodge remarks, 'that not only Psalms, but *hymns*, as distinct compositions, also were employed.' As to the Septuagint use of the term, when Isaiah would predict the glorious triumphs of the gospel, he exclaims—'Sing unto the Lord a new song (*humnon* or hymn), and his praise from the ends of the earth.' Chapter xlii. 10. The Greek is very expressive—'*Hymn* unto the Lord a *new hymn*.' The hymn immediately follows, and though not found in 'the Book of Psalms,' Isaiah exhorts to sing it, including, of course, all similar hymns; an exhortation or command just as binding upon the New Testament church as any requirement to 'sing Psalms' which is found in the book of that name."

We shall not follow the order of the statements in this closing part of the paragraph quoted. We shall notice first, the least important part thrown upon our attention. The main points last.

The reference to Isaiah xlii. 10, is a fair specimen of the use of the scripture testimony through the entire argument for a human psalmody. The Septuagint, translating Isaiah here, says—" *Hymn* unto the Lord a *new hymn*." This *new hymn*, not being found in the Book of Psalms, is, with "all *similar*" in the Bible, by command of Isaiah, to be sung in the New Testament churches. That is, fortunately the Septuagint, translating the Hebrew, *shir* and its cognate, says—" *Hymn* a *new hymn;* " and from the very sweet euphony of the sound—" *Hymn* a *new hymn*," hymn-singing is proved by Isaiah's command, as translated by the Septuagint!

Moreover, we are very particularly told this *new hymn*

is not in the Book of Psalms, but certainly found in Isaiah, and that *it* and *similar* are meant. Then, Isaiah's *hymns* being *inspired writings* of the Bible, we seem to have made one step in the progress of the argument towards proving the right of singing the inspired songs of the Bible outside the Book of Psalms. But is this even one step in the way of proving the divine right of a very different thing—the Presbyterian way of *making uninspired* hymns, and by authority of the "supreme judicatory" authorizing the poems of Watts, Moore, etc., to be sung?

Again, this little attempt to make an argument, without the weight of a feather, out of a mere verbal criticism, shows the desperate demand for some shadow of a Bible argument. Yes, we are told, "the Greek is *very expressive!*"—"*Hymn* a *new hymn.*" Of what is this a translation? The original Hebrew, in Isa. xlii. 10, *shir*, the Septuagint finds, in the opening of the Canticles, *shir shirim*, and translates by *asma asmaton*, "song of songs." Why not, to be *very expressive*, say—*Hymn of Hymns*, which is Solomon's? Sometimes Septuagint verbal *criticism* means *sillyism!* How convincing the proof for making and singing uninspired hymns! We are about where we started in seeking our brethren's Bible argument for their New Testament way. Beyond argument for using "other inspired songs," we have not seen the shadow of testimony.

THE LEADING POINT OF ASSUMPTION IN THIS PARAGRAPH, ITS IDENTITIES, AND DEDUCTIONS THEREFROM.

Any appearance of argument, in the paragraph before us, is in its identifying the apostle's "rebuke," in 1 Cor. xiv. 26, with his command in Eph. v. 19, and Col. iii. 16. The Psalms, hymns and spiritual songs, the objects of the approval and command, being of the same *class*—the fruits of the gifts of the Spirit—as the object of the "rebuke," they were all inspired writings beyond the Book of Psalms. The Septuagint's *very expressive* translation of Isaiah furnishes the proof. Or, bringing out the concealed conclusion, as in other instances, after a circuitous travel, diverting the mind from the premises, the conclusion is ambiguously pronounced. The process may be stated thus—as the apostolical church was endowed with extraordinary spiritual gifts, among which was that of enabling the whole membership to compose inspired songs; the church now, following the example of apostolical times, may, in her "supreme judicatory," do what the church did by the gift of inspiration, authorize the use of uninspired hymns, not only outside the Book of Psalms, but outside the inspired songs of the Bible. Can we be mistaken here in stating assumption, argument or conclusion?

We have noticed, in chapter iii., this high church prerogative, so arrogantly assumed. We shall now trace the process by which the conclusion is reached. In analyzing the process of the argument before us, we may notice—

1. The *assumption* that the *Psalms* of 1 Cor. xiv. 26 were inspired—they were the fruits of the extraordinary gifts of the Spirit.

2. The *assumption* that the Psalms, hymns and spiritual songs of Eph. v. 19 and Col. iii. 16 were of the same class, inspired Psalms, "as well as those of David."

3. The *assumption* that in Eph. and Col. Paul exhorts to sing the songs thus composed under the Spirit of inspiration—impromptu Psalms, hymns and spiritual songs, given by the Spirit for the occasion.

4. The *assumption* that these examples, and Paul's command authorize the Presbyterian way—the composition of uninspired poets, authorized by the prerogative of the "supreme judicatory" of the church.

The question is suggested here, as in all cases of illogical reasoning, are the premises well laid? Is the conclusion warranted by the premises? If, for premises, we have unreasonable or false assumptions, and then from these we have forced and illogical conclusions, must not the argument be utter failure?

In Corinth "every one had a Psalm." Without a miracle how could every one have a Psalm, if every one of these illiterate people, as is assumed, *made* his own Psalm? But to meet the case, as on the other hand assumed—"few able to read"—a miracle is assumed for the occasion and for the argument. The gift of inspiration is given to a whole congregation of illiterate people—all inspired to make extempore Psalms, and sing them! That cuts the gordian knot. Grand as the immaculate conception! A miracle by which every one was full of inspired Psalms, overflowing, so that when the apostle admonished to "sing," they all understood him to mean, not to sing anything known, but, by their miraculous gift, to make for the occasion; just to open their inspired lips, and all at once, in universal jargon, Psalms would flow in streams out of all their inspired mouths, each differing in matter and sentiment from the other; or, why inspire all, when otherwise one inspired poet would have sufficed, and Paul's "rebuke" been avoided?

This is the argument:

"Besides, when the apostle rebukes the Corinthians as follows: 'Every one of you hath a Psalm,' the common interpretation is, that these *Psalms* were the fruits of the gifts of the Spirit then bestowed on the membership of the Christian church." This being imagined and assumed in argument, one stretch farther of imagination beyond what is written, and the case is made out thus: "Then, why might not the same Divine influence have been found at Ephesus and Colosse?" Of course, here, unable to furnish the shadow of an argument to prove the truth of an affirmation, the demand to prove a negative—"Why might not?" We shall state *why not* in regard to both affirmations. God, by his Spirit, never gave any such gifts for any such purposes, both disgraceful and scandalous, subjecting the actors to public "rebuke." God is not the Author of confusion. But this whole business of every one coming to the worship of God with a Psalm, as stated, was confusion not of God.

We may be asked: If the Bible Psalms were brought, and no miraculous, or extraordinary, gifts in the case, what better upon this hypothesis? Would not the confusion have been the same, and as justly exposed to rebuke?

We answer—

1. This is the only reasonable hypothesis on which the membership *could* have merited "rebuke."

2. This is the only reasonable hypothesis on which Paul *could* be justified in administering the "rebuke."

3. On this hypothesis the Holy Spirit stands exonerated from all responsibility for confusion or exposure to "rebuke."

The disorderly people, under wrong impulses, were alone to blame. They did all this through their own misguided and ignorant zeal. They abused the order of God's house. As any church members might do this, and the Holy Spirit not be the Author of the confusion, or of the *animus* that prompted it! We say, the Holy Spirit did not give that afflatus, that gift, or fruit of such gift, that led to such disorder and scandal. On the other hand, if those illiterate people were all under the special and extraordinary influences of the Spirit, moved by the Spirit of inspiration, all at the same time, all in the same way, to act those extempore performances, the Spirit was then the Author of the confusion. And what business had even Paul to "rebuke" either the Holy Spirit or his fruits? For, we are called to remember that all this is charged to "the fruits of the gifts of the Spirit *then* bestowed." "By their fruits ye shall know them."

The whole argument drawn from these passages for hymn-making, by the entire membership of the church, belongs to inventive imagination, in the absence of all Bible argument. By the consent of all, these churches in question had and knew the Bible, and must have known the Bible Psalms, hymns, and spiritual songs. That they had any other, knew any other, or used any other, no mortal can furnish the shadow of affirmative proof. To demand of us negative proof is concession to the badness of the cause, affirming without evidence

THE ARGUMENT FROM SCRIPTURE EXAMPLE.

We leave the *three* texts considered, from which our friends draw direct authority, by command, to *make* and *sing* uninspired hymns, and turn to their *pattern* texts, *after which* they *make* and sing them.

Approved example is certainly a scriptural form of establishing Divine authority. But caution is suggested here. Approved example for one thing, or one class of things, may not be good authority for a very different thing, or for a very different class of things.

Bear with us in making a quotation from one of the latest issues of the champion of this controversy, whose spear-handle is like a weaver's beam, and in whose eyes the weapons of his antagonists are as the slingstones of mere boys:

"For example, THERE IS NOT A SOLITARY INSTANCE IN THE NEW TESTAMENT OF THE SINGING OF THE PSALMS OF DAVID IN LITERAL FORM. On the contrary, the Apostles used the Book of Psalms in quite a different mode in the only *two* cases in which they employed them in social praise. One of these is Luke xix. 38. The disciples took part of a verse from Psalm cxviii., but sung it with alterations adapted to their circumstances. The *second* case is in Acts iv. 24. The beginning of the second Psalm is sung by Peter, John, and their company—then an addition, in the beginning—then a narrative of what David spoke—then an application to Herod, Pontius Pilate, etc.,—then an enlargement by considering the hand of God in the whole, and finally the song concludes with desires suited to their circumstances. This is an inspired pattern for making New Testament Psalms. It groups together parts of the Psalms along with other inspired matter, just as Dr. Watts and Presbyterians do." In another connection it is added—"in composing hymns, agreeably to the example in Acts iv. 24, of a song of praise gathered."

It is remarkable how much dogmatical assurance we have from our brethren in all their efforts to furnish evidence of the truth of their leading affirmative—The Divine authority for making uninspired hymns for divine worship. The fact that the New Testament *records no instance* of singing "in literal form," proves that making in *unliteral* form is a divine right! Paul and Silas *sang*. The record don't say they sung the 46th Psalm, nor quote for our eyes; therefore they made a hymn for the occasion; and we are gravely asked to prove they did not! Is there not as much evidence that the Psalms of the Bible were sung in *literal* form, in all the instances in which singing God's praise in worship is referred to in the New Testament, as that these two are examples of *hymn-making?* For, in neither of these is there shadow of evidence that there was hymn-making at all. In one, not the shadow of evidence that there was singing, even. Of this again.

We are here told that Watts and Presbyterians do

"just as" apostles did in these instances. Now, we know certainly just what Watts and Presbyterians do; for their ways and doings are before our eyes, and before the world. And we know, as well, they do not even attempt to do what the apostles did, as our friends say. Watts composed, by his "poetical talent," uninspired matter. He did not "group together Psalms and *other inspired matter.*" He did not pretend, even, to translate. He may have sometimes quoted from the Bible, as from any other book. But here, in the instances referred, every word of the Psalm, or song, or hymn, or matter composed and recorded by the apostles, is certainly the inspired word of God. Did the apostles and Watts do the same thing? We might leave the matter here.

Face to face we shall meet, with our friends, these "two cases" of "inspired pattern."

First, the one from Luke xix. 38. Come, now, reader, with us to the hill over against this scene recorded by Luke. Let us adjust our camera. Let us take a deliberate panorama view of that life-scene, as it passed on that day of Christ's entrance into Jerusalem, and that grand procession of apostles, and disciples, and multitudes of believers, and men, and women, and children, and confused mass of friends and the unfriendly—such a march! Such an excited mass! Such a tumultuous throng and noisy multitude! Such, perhaps, Jerusalem never saw!

What are they all doing? See them, strewing palms, and garments all along the way! All, all shouting huzzas and hosannas! On, on moves the jubilant, shouting throng! Every eye turned to the son of David. The multitudes before and behind, shouting at the top of their voices! Lo! Just then, some poet laureate is seen in conspicuous position, on some elevation, with reporter's apparatus, and with one wave of his poetic wand, stays and stills the tumult and the march. Then and there, in time for briefness, unparalleled in the history of stenography, he gathers from Ps. cxviii., and from various other passages of holy writ, arranges, and writes—as in those days of impromptu hymn-making, they could write and dispatch business—and reads out line by line, to the silent, listening, waiting multitude, before and behind, every word, and distinctly, so as to be heard by all engaged in this "social praise."—And then, after being examined, *amended* and approved by the Master on the colt, in whom, *at that time*, was lodged all the power of *supreme judicatory, now*, the Presbyterian way—all, all sang this new-made, New Testament, uninspired Psalm! Made, too, *just as Presbyterians do now!* An apostolical New Testament hymn!—Our friends say it was a Psalm! And we don't know whether it was psalm, hymn, or song! For the Bible don't tell us what it was; and our friends had affirmed, and promised the proof that while Psalm might mean inspired Psalm, yet hymn and song mean human composition, and here we have the example, the *pattern* for *making* them.—Here, made impromptu, for the occasion, and "beyond controversy, sung in *social praise.*"

Now, good friends, seriously, when you are done looking for yourselves at this pattern picture, this example for making uninspired hymns, by poet and supreme judicatory, ask yourselves—Wherein are the example and copy like? Does anybody believe that uninspired poets ever composed odes, poems, psalms, hymns, songs in any such way, in any such tumult, in any such circumstances, and impromptu? —Out on parade, in procession and triumphal march amid the shouts and huzzas of a confused, moving throng? Instanter? But if that were not a sober, calm, thoughtful hymn-composing occasion, and one on which the hymn-making multitude and apostles were not in hymn-composing mood, what then? What *is* here spread out before our scene-contemplating view?

Some things were not exhibited, nor exemplified on that very exciting march and entrance into Jerusalem.

1. That was not family worship; though in such worship some Christians do engage in *social praise*.

2. It was not a prayer-meeting, since Christ did not, thus mounted, attend the *upper room* meetings "with the women, the doors being shut;" "though Christians there do usually unite in *social praise*."

3. It was not the Synagogue worship; for that was not like a portable tent that could be pitched anywhere on a march like this, just at the entrance of Jerusalem.

4. It was not the temple service; nor yet, any kind of religious service, or gathering where the social worship of God was known to be observed. It must have been some *sui generis* occasion, calling for this *sui generis* Presbyterian way of uninspired hymn-making, impromptu, and singing with the same breath! Illustrious example! Yes —to be copied to the end of the world!

To say that the impassioned, impromptu shouts of the multitude in that extraordinary triumphal entrance of Christ into Jerusalem, is a pattern for anything in the instituted ordinances of religious worship, is not only a trifling with religious things, but ludicrous. Let us then see, what did occur on that march.

1. The occasion itself was extraordinary, and unlike anything in the ordinary worship of God in his church; and cannot exemplify the ordinance of *social praise*.

2. The multitudes, led by the excitement—or if it may please—the inspiration of the extraordinary occasion prompting to shout huzzas, were led by no one as an official leader in Divine worship; their minds not solemnized, or even thinking of any kind of formal religious worship

at all, they were perhaps only irregularly shouting aloud and repeating Bible phrases memorized, or caught up one from another.

3. Or, many in the multitudes may have broken out into singing from *memory;* from these others might join in the song, and so shout and sing aloud.

4. We have here only the inspired historian's brief outline of what was done, said or sung. That outline narrative, neither by Luke nor one of the other Evangelists, hints even that the things said or sung were composed by the Apostles as uninspired hymns, and then and there, as from their pen, for the first time repeated and sung by the multitude in *social praise.*

5. And then—every word here recorded by Luke, whether psalm, hymn, or song—whether said, recited, vociferated or sung, is divinely inspired. It may be *like* many another thing—may be a *pattern* for many things—one thing can never be said of it, with truth or good sense—that this is "just what Dr. Watts and Presbyterians do," in making New Testament uninspired hymns and songs.

Absolutely, neither Watts nor any Presbyterian ever made hymns for social praise, in any such tumultuous throng. Nor did any such throng ever shout out, in unison, extempore, uninspired hymns to be sung in "social praise;" nor do hymns spontaneously make themselves in any such way! Rather, were not every one of your hymns made deliberately at your desks, pen in hand, brain and mind composed, all their powers taxed, hushed and subdued in sober thought? Brethren, you may as well quote as divine authority for uninspired hymn-making, "as Presbyterians do," these words of Dan. iii. 23, "*And these three men, Shadrach, Meshech and Abednego fell down.*"—We are willing to meet, with all serene gravity, every serious and grave argument. But when you deal in ludicrous fiction, don't expect unremitting long faces, or "put-on" gravity.

The champion of the cause of impromptu hymn-making on the march, amid procession and throng, by a little shifting of the scene, may tell us that the disciples had this triumphal psalm all previously collected, compiled, "grouped," arranged, prepared for the occasion, and previously adapted to the circumstances. A good beginning for the poetic illiterate fishermen! And then, the learned Physician, Luke, only gives an outline sketch of the scenes and occurrences of that memorable day; and consequently as the uninspired psalm was not intended for the sacred record, it is not *extant!*

This is about as plausible a fiction as any other invented to sustain the cause of this wonderful "pattern" theory of uninspired psalm-making, or *inspired* psalm-making, "*as Presbyterians* do." Since after all, as the psalm was grouped, in its being lost no loss can be sustained—for we are gravely told in these remarkable words—"This is an inspired pattern for making New Testament psalms. It groups together parts of psalms, along with other *inspired* matter, just as Dr. Watts and Presbyterians do."

Then, there was nothing in it but what is in the Bible somewhere, "other inspired matter, and the cxviii. Psalm." Quotations from scripture, would be scripture still. Yet there seems to be a great loss—for here in this "pattern" lies the secret of the art of "using scripturally the Psalms." How, or on what principle, was this grouping together conducted? Inspired matter grouped from all parts of the Bible, and appended to the defective Psalms, not one of which was fit for Apostles to use "IN LITERAL FORMS," is, in these "two cases" only, found in the New Testament. And now, the very pattern itself lost! Only a meagre sketch of some of its parts *extant!* Lost! Like the *Lost*

Arts, this "pattern" psalm, lost with all the New Testament psalms, sung at Corinth, Ephesus and Colosse, said to be used by the Christians for many, many centuries, must be a loss.

To have exhumed from the historical debris of the ages *this one* lost psalm—this inspired and yet uninspired "pattern" psalm of which all Presbyterian psalms are exact copies—this psalm, which, it may be presumed, was called by the first singers, "*Hymn of the Grand Entrance*"—this would be the *desideratum!* O, what inscrutable providence has hid from the ages the *better* psalms, these apostolical psalms of "pattern" value, and yet preserved so carefully and transmitted through the centuries these *inferior* Bible Psalms, not one of which seems to be fit for social praise, till their *literal form* shall be changed and a regenerating process pass over them by Presbyterian hands. Could our brethren sing Luke ii. 9-14, *in literal form*, without grouping in their way?

THE SECOND PATTERN CASE FOR HYMN-MAKING, Acts iv. 24.

This *second case*, of the only *two*, in which the Apostles employed the Book of Psalms "in social praise," "as Presbyterians do," is the more important as it is the last witness summoned to prove for our brethren the Divine authority for making and singing, in the formal worship of God, uninspired hymns. If this fail them, they have not, in a single text in the Bible, the shadow of authority for their doctrine on Psalmody. Let us patiently hear their own use of this witness on the stand. They say:

"The beginning of the Second Psalm is sung by Peter, John, and their company—then an addition, in the beginning—then a narrative of what David spoke—then an application to Herod, Pontius Pilate, etc., then an enlargement, by considering the hand of God in the whole, and finally the song concludes with desires suited to their circumstances. This is an inspired pattern for making New Testament psalms."

This is the sum of the evidence, summed up by the skill of a practised tactician, in which there is not one word of truth as warranted by the testimony. We have seldom, if ever, noticed in the same narrow space more antic carricature of the word of God, greater perversion and misapplication, more ludicrous statements and assumptions, more desperate torture of the plain statements of the Bible, by wresting and dragging them violently into the cause of a controversy which should never appeal to the Scriptures at all, but to popular feeling, popular sentiment, popular taste only, whence all its argument really comes. Ludicrous, we said; yes, for 1. To say that here is a *case* of *singing* an uninspired psalm, made for the occasion, by one or by a company, by somebody or nobody, is *ludicrous*.

2. To say that is a *pattern case* of Presbyterian psalm-making, is *more ludicrous* still.

3. The *description* given of this new psalm-*singing* and *making* at the same time, by the same company, is *most ludicrous of all—is sublimely ludicrous*.

In the light of common sense, let us look after the plain facts, as stated in Acts iv. 24–31. We have in this passage a plain case, plainly stated of extempore *social prayer*, just that much *expressed*, and not one word more, instead of *social praise-making*. Common sense reads this in this passage.

1. In the affirmation stated in the very words of the original Greek, *Epo*, used in the 25th verse, means to *say*, never to sing. This verb is used in the New Testament about 1,000 times; here tortured to sing.

Didomai, in the 29th verse, which means to *grant*, is used some 400 times in the New Testament, and never once to sing. *Deamai*, in the 31st verse, is used twenty-one times always meaning to *pray*, never to sing.

2. Our translators faithfully render every word to mean prayer and not singing; and, indeed, every word in the entire paragraph, besides those specified, to accord with this specific meaning. Read them, "And said," said what? "Lord, thou art God"—beginning with adoration. Then, "Now, Lord, behold," using in the body of the prayer the veritable language of supplication. And still more definitely they *said*, " Grant unto thy servants." Then, as if to settle all doubt or evasion, the record, as translated, says, "And when they had prayed "—when they had done praying—when prayer was over—" the place was shaken." Then,

3. The commentators governed by common sense all agree that this was a *case* of *social prayer*. And, more: even hymn-singing commentators agree here, and we cite no other, Gill, Scott, Henry, The Comprehensive, etc., all agree with us. Not one of them gives a hint of uninspired hymn-making or singing. This is reserved for a desperate champion of the controversial quill and endorsers, and for the desperate cause of finding—pardon us—of *inventing* some form of Scriptural countenance for such calling. But what do the princes commentators of our own brethren say of this " example of *inspired pattern* " for uninspired Psalm-making? What do their own Barnes and their own Jacobus say? These are recent commentators. Their issues have appeared since the *invention* of this " pattern " plan of hymn-making. These authors are not visionary scribblers. They were not engaged in the professional business of wresting the Scriptures into shapeless carricatures, ludicrous enough to excite the laughter of the Infidel into a roar.

Barnes says, commenting on Acts iv. 24–31:

" To lift up the voice *to God*, means simply, they prayed

to him." Yes, "*simply* means," what is obvious to every mind free from partizan bias. At the close of the paragraph, he says on verse 31:

"And when they had prayed."—" The event which followed was regarded by them as an evidence that God heard their prayer."—" A similar instance of an answer to prayer by an earthquake is recorded in Acts xvi. 25."

Jacobus on the passage begins with a caption thus:

"The Prayer of the Whole Church."—" It is plain that some one of them led in prayer, in which all the assembly joined. It is said, They lifted up their voice—one voice leading many hearts—' with one accord.'" Again, " The prayer addresses Jehovah as absolute Governor." Again, he says, commenting on Peter's prayer, verse 26: "And grant." " They do not pray for the destruction of their enemies." But they pray only for what their Great High-Priest had asked. " This accordingly was granted them as the substance of their prayer." "All they asked for was the Divine signature to their work." On verse 31st:

"Result of the Prayer."—" Immediately, and as a manifest answer to their prayers, not the earth only, but also heaven shook that place of prayer." The next chapter is, indeed, a wonderful record of what they were enabled to do in direct answer to this prayer."

What a contrast betwixt the views of these candid commentators, who had no end to subserve but simple truth, and the views of controversialists, whose object is to mould a pattern for uninspired hymn-making. A contrast as bold as betwixt candor and chicanery, sense and caricature, of the plain teachings of the word of God.

The *second* and *more ludicrous* aspect of this caricature—this pattern case of Presbyterian hymn-*making:*

Here curiosity prompts the inquiry, if not the smile, *Who* gathered, grouped, arranged, composed, penned, and set to music this new-born psalm, in singing which a whole congregation joined? And then how? The composing of praise, or psalm-making, by a multitude with one accord, is an absurdity, contrary to the very nature of the ordinance of praise. Song is composed by a single writer, whose pen commits to paper for the eye. Through the eye upon the page many minds may be brought to praise with one accord. This implies the pre-existence of the composition, its commitment to the book, then the use of the book.—All these forming means and mediums through and by which minds and voices act with one accord. Such composing and penning, *en masse*, and then concordant singing impromptu, could not have occurred without a miracle, and the miracle useless and without a moral. It could not be a "pattern" for Presbyterian hymn-making, and consequently of use to nobody.

The *third* and *most ludicrous* aspect of this Bible caricature: The graphic descriptive analysis of the composition, by poets in company, of this *pattern* psalm. Peter, and all the company, *in the very act of* lifting up their voice in singing the beginning of the Second Psalm ("the literal form" not being suitable), they all, just then, continuing the song, *make*—" then an addition to the beginning." An addition to what? In the beginning of the Second Psalm —before the first verse or after the second? "Then a narrative of what David spoke." But this narrative added to the addition added to the beginning, was the veritable two verses themselves of the Second Psalm, which they had just sung in *verbal form* before commencing the making of this New Testament, uninspired, pattern psalm. "Then the application to Herod, Pontius Pilate," etc. In sermons the application usually closes the discourse. But this was extraordinary. After the application, a little more finishing of this "finished" pattern composition. "Then an enlargement "—not large enough after application, addition and narrative, a finality must be appended as a voluntary to complete this model of all human compositions. "And, finally, the song concludes with desires suited to the circumstances. This is an inspired pattern for making New Testament psalms."

Now, in all this process of singing a Psalm of David, in amending the Psalm, in composing for present New Testament use by a whole *company*—not a jar—everything in model unison—every brain beat with every other brain, and thought responded to thought, and all kept time—every pen moved gracefully as one, and by one mind controlled—every voice in perfect concord, " all with one accord." Such unison earth seldom enjoys.

REFLECTIONS. In examining the leading testimony on which our brethren rely as "stronghold" evidence to establish their Divine authority for making and singing uninspired hymns, we are induced to apply more formal exegetical and analytical scrutiny to their proof-texts, and a closer examination into the character and design of this meeting.

Was this impromptu meeting of Acts iv. 24, a "committee on the Revision of the Psalms?" Was it a Christian "singing circle," met to sing and cultivate sacred music? Was it a meeting suddenly called—a surprise meeting of the released apostles, Peter and John, and the company of the disciples, in which, on hearing from the released prisoners, they turned their gathering into an extempore prayer-meeting? Can there be any kind of question in regard to the character of the meeting, or the leading features of its exercises? It was simply an impromptu prayer-meeting. It was not among its dreams, even, to *make* new psalms, or gather, group, and amend old ones. That they had, in this meeting, the other ordinary exercises of the prayer-meeting, may be; so to suppose may not be absurd. They may have read a chapter of the Bible. They may have sung the second Psalm. They may have "spoken one to another," "exhorted one another," as in ordinary prayer-meetings. We cannot prove they did not. We leave all this negative business to our friends, who depend on "why nots" for argument. We can prove they *prayed*, for the text *affirms* it.

Jacobus, besides giving his own views, refers to the opinion of some other commentator, and says:

"It is supposed that the whole church *sang* the 'words' ('verbal form'?) of the Second Psalm, and prayed, and that *then Peter* made an application of the Psalm (explained after singing?) to their present case *in the words here recorded.*"

In the references before us, we have *three distinct statements* of the character of the assembly recorded in Acts iv. 24:

1. Our hymn-singing commentators, Barnes, Jacobus, etc., as we have seen, say we have "prayer" here—"THE PRAYER OF THE WHOLE CHURCH."

2. Jacobus hints that some have supposed it to be a prayer-meeting, in which they sang, talked, and prayed; and that in singing they *used* the "*words* of the *Second Psalm*"!

3. Our trained champions, professional advocates, in the cause of an uninspired psalmody, say: "This is an inspired pattern for making New Testament psalms—just as Dr. Watts and Presbyterians do." "There is not a single instance in the New Testament of the singing of a Psalm of David in a literal form." And then, "Only *two* cases in which they employed them in social praise."

These hymn-singing brethren can settle their conflicting views among themselves. All taken together, they prove nothing of authority for Presbyterian hymn-making; rather, they give damaging hints, neutralizing the whole probation. To sing a Psalm of David, and to sing the very "words" thereof—to sing the veritable "verbal form"—is to look, at least a little, toward inspired psalm-singing in early New Testament times. This they did not mean to prove by their "stronghold" evidence, affirming the Divine authority for a very different thing from that which they designed to make it speak.

Brethren: We are not yet prepared to follow you in your "way" of hymn-making and singing. You must, to prove affirmatively in a matter of Divine worship, furnish us something more rational than that the company of Acts iv. 24 was a mere committee on psalmody, for the revision of the inspired Psalms of the Bible, grouping inspired writings for New Testament use in the praise of God.

We thank you, nevertheless. You give us the best you have. Till you find better we shall ask to be excused from following you. We shall stand still in the *way* of our God.

CHAPTER V.

THE SCOTTISH VERSION OF THE BOOK OF PSALMS VINDICATED AS A TRANSLATION.

Importance attached to the question of translation—No other version subjected to such extreme criticism—Mistranslation defined—Charges of gross mistranslations examined—The First, the Sixteenth, and the Sixty-ninth Psalms vindicated from charges of gross mistranslation—Mistranslations in the prose Bible compared with the worst examples in Rouse—Charges of patch-work and paraphrase of Rouse examined—Manufactured patches charged to the account of Rouse—Specimens of similar and greater patches in our English version—Various classes of specimens—Use of Divine names, when not in the original, charged as a prejudice against Rouse—Superabundance of similar instances in our prose Bible.

THE Scottish Version of the Book of Psalms has, we are inclined to believe, been the object of more furious attack, and the subject of more severe and extreme criticism, than all the translations of all the books of the Bible besides; including all the hundreds of tongues into which they have been translated in modern times. The true friends of the Bible—friends of its universal circulation, adoption, and use in everything for which it is "suited" and designed—friends of its universal influence among all nations and tongues—will be slow to attack translations long sanctioned and used by the church of Christ. Here is a translation sanctioned, not by a committee of civilians, called by Royal prerogative, but by one of the most evangelical and venerable of all the Assemblies that have convened in all Christendom for two and a quarter centuries. Here is a translation of one of the books of the Bible, prepared and sanctioned by the Church of Scotland in the days of her learning, her power, her glory. Rutherford, Henderson, Gillespie, Baillie, Douglass, were there. "There were giants in those days." The most evangelical churches of Protestantism have, ever since those golden days, used this translation. Some of the best scholars of the last two centuries have recognized this translation as worthy of a place among the versions of the books of the Bible. From *one single quarter* have all the fierce assaults come—from partizan controversialists.

Here, and now, we design not even an attempt to ward off all the strokes of the enemies of this version, or offer for it a formal and elaborate vindication. We have here but little more than *one point* to make: *Our Scottish version is a translation.* We have, in the meantime, one word of caution for our friends and readers on the subject of our Scottish version of the Book of Psalms: Remember the maxim, Do not throw stones from glass houses. Or, deal gently and *candidly* with the subject of Bible translations: the more so in this age of missions, of Bibles, of Bible translation, and Bible circulation.

In making *this one point*, we have to say: It would be very easy to turn this weapon of severe criticism, so adroitly handled by the opponents of this version, upon the translation of King James, and in the same way, and so play into the hand of the Infidel, as our friends are incautiously doing. These attacks upon a scripture psalmody might, in *manner* of the opponent, have been repelled long since but for repugnance to the use of such weapons.

Here is the assault and the tactics; and here is our *one point*, to *parry the blow aimed at our version.* Let us state these. A few blemishes, of a certain kind, are found in this version. These are magnified, distorted, misnamed, and many added, not in the version at all. Then, the *whole* is branded as a mere paraphrase—a piece of patchwork—no version at all, having no claims to be recognized as the word of God, as a scripture psalmody, and nothing more than human composition, just like Watts' imitation. This principle of criticism, applied by our friends to this version, pronounces upon our Bible in common use, and almost certainly upon the Bible in every language into which it has ever been translated. Not one of them all is without blemish, or mark of human error in translating. Our own, among the very best extant, cannot, for an hour, stand this ordeal of the unreasonable and monstrous test applied to the version in question. The Septuagint, the translation of the Bible used as the word of God in the days of Christ and his apostles, and by the church now for twenty centuries past, and thus far passed unchallenged—a worse translation than the Scottish version—could not for a moment stand the ordeal applied here.

Do our friends really assume that King James' translation is perfect, and an honest test-rule by which to pronounce upon every other? From this stand-point do they view our version as a paper wall, through which they can furiously dash like a wild bull, and, passing through it, presume they can toss it into fragments high in air? Gentlemen! we live in the nineteenth century. The Bashan breed are extinct. You may have missed your calling and your coat of mail.

For nearly a century the leading advocates of a human psalmody have found fault with the Book of Psalms itself, and on the ground of its unfitness for New Testament worship. Even apologies for the hard sayings of Dr. Watts disparaging this part of the word of God, admit that a *part* of the Book of Psalms, without reference to Rouse, or any other version, is "adapted to sink the devotion" of Christians at the present time. More recently controversial tactics have been materially changed. While it is not so popular to attack, directly, any part of the Bible, it is deemed comparatively safe to assail a metrical version of the Psalms, denouncing it as a paraphrase, a patch-work, no version at all, because it fails to be word for word with our prose translation.

It will be well, just here, to have in our minds a definite understanding of the rules by which honorable men judge of the merits of translations; the various kinds of translations and mistranslations; their respective merits and demerits; and especially the question, whether any translation can, in any proper sense, be recognized as the word of God.

There are various kinds and degrees of mistranslations. There is the *gross* and palpable kind, rendering a word, or sentence, by a word, or words, of a different or apposite meaning; as *Easter* for *Pascha*, a palpable mistranslation. There is a form of mistranslation where the meaning of the original is not fully brought out and transferred to the vernacular, or when more is transferred than is in the original. It is a blemish in translation when it is too liberal, when there are too many expletives, too much expansion of the thought, too much repetition, or when approximating to comment or paraphrase. The *first* of these is the most objectionable, the *last* the least offensive and dangerous. The one leads from the way altogether, the other only obscures.

Candor will admit that all translations have their blemishes. And, like them all, our metrical Psalms have theirs. This we acknowledge, and this we are laboring to remedy. What number, or degree, of blemishes may destroy the claims of a version to a place among recognized translations, it is not our place to fix the line, or adjust the scale. This our brethren should not have overlooked when commencing their work of weighing versions in the scales of a translation; it was properly their work, as a logical conclusion, from their high assumptions of judiciary prerogative over versions. We have this to say here, however: there are many translations having a long and unquestioned recognition, some of which have had a place in the church for nearly two thousand years. Hundreds have, in modern times, taken rank among versions, and are finding their way, as the recognized word of God, to all nations, kindreds, peoples and tongues on earth. Have we been mistaken here? Are we sending the heathen bread, or a stone? Are we sending them the scriptures, the veritable word of the living God, or patch-work and paraphrase only?—mere notes and comments? Let us know. There is a standard. Established use sometimes becomes a law. In applying the standard, the original text, shall we adopt the rule of our brethren, one that will sweep every translation extant from the catalogue? And are we to submit to such a rule, and coolly permit our version to be put under ban, while no better, perhaps inferior, hold their position unchallenged? To this we demur. And still more: we refuse to be tried and condemned by any other version of equal, or greater, defects.

In regard to the *first* and *gross* kind of mistranslation, we challenge the most rigid scrutiny.

CHARGE, AGAINST ROUSE, OF GROSS MISTRANSLATION AND ERROR REPELLED.

We here *assert:* There is not a single instance of the *first* and *gross* kind of mistranslation in our Scottish version, from beginning to end, except in one or two, where the Septuagint, or our prose version, is followed. On the other hand, we concede that, like the Septuagint, and like our prose Bible, there are many instances of expletives, expansions, repetitions to excess, demonstrating that it might be improved. These conceded imperfections no more destroy its claims to a place among versions, than the imperfections of our common Bible prove that it is not the word of God.

We now appeal to the standard.

In the very opening of our version, and in the very *first* line of the *First* Psalm, we meet the charge of *gross* mistranslation. Thus—

"The blunders of Rouse, in making David say the true Christian, in his experience of this life, 'hath perfect blessedness'—which implies *perfect holiness,* and teaches the error of sinless perfection."

We reply to this bold, yet silly, sophomoric charge in the language of a scholar, a divine, and hymn-singing commentator—Dr. J. A. Alexander, late of Princeton, N. J.:

"The description opens with a kind of admiring exclamation—(*Oh!*) *the blessedness of the man!* The plural form of the original (*felicities, or happinesses*), if anything more than grammatical idiom, in our language may denote *fullness* and variety of happiness, as if he had said, *How completely happy is the man!*"

In addition, we notice, "Ashre," the word in controversy, is a *noun*. So it is in Rouse. An abstract noun in the plural form—"blessednesses." The prose Bible gives an adjective—"blessed," and adds an auxiliary verb—"is." Bishop Louth says the plural noun here is like the Latin vocative plural, and has the force of an adjective in the superlative degree; as, O, the inexpressible blessedness of the man! So, Dr. Alexander—"complete blessedness." Now, had Rouse said—

"That man hath 'happiness complete,' who walketh not astray," would he and Alexander have been antagonistic? Again, had Rouse said—

"That man hath 'blessedness' *complete*, who walketh not astray,"

would there yet be antagonism? And now, as it is, how broad, deep, wide, the difference betwixt *complete* and *perfect?* Does complete happiness imply complete holiness in this life, and so teach the error of sinless perfection here? Not so fast, just here, friends of Dr. Alexander! Neither Lowth, nor Alexander, nor Rouse, nor David, nor the Holy Spirit in the Psalm, teaches that "the Christian hath in this life" any such sinless perfection. Had not our friends committed the incomparably greater blunder—*first*, of casting *Christ* out of the Psalm, as their cause imperatively demands, and *second*, of applying descriptions of character as primarily belonging to the Christian, which so belong to "no mere man since the fall," they could not have so exposed their weakness and prejudice. More, by-and-by, of the spirit and principle brought to the surface here in this desperate attack upon this precious Psalm, in which there is so much of Christ, and in which our brethren, for the sake of consistency and their cause, must see nothing of the *blessed* Saviour.

Attacks upon Rouse, like all other attacks upon a scripture psalmody, will do very well for loose declamation, so long as there is no grappling with principle or facts. But when Rouse is brought face to face with other versions, and their defects laid open before the final test of all translations, the whole controversy assumes a very different aspect. Put other translations upon their own defence, pressed by the claims of law and standard, and the issue presents a very different character. And here, in the *First Psalm*, let these unreasonable assaults upon our version find a striking illustration. Because the word "*perfect*" is there used, the charges come down like snow flakes—rather like hail stones—thick, and fast, and chilling. "Gross error in doctrine," "mistranslation" of monstrous kind, charges enough to freeze the heart and close the lips of any credulous worshipper who could for a moment give heed to the damaging aspersions. Few arguments against our version have any more sense or weight than this, therefore we dwell upon it.

Why, truly, Rouse says "*perfect*," and the Psalms are denounced. Now, if this is error in Rouse, so gross that his Psalms are untrue, and patch-work, what of that Book which reads, "Noah was a just man, and *perfect* in his generation;" which reads, "My servant Job, a *perfect* and an upright man;" which reads, "Mark the *perfect* and behold the upright;" which reads, "That they may shoot in secret at the *perfect*;" which reads, "I will behave myself wisely in a *perfect* way;" which reads, "He that walketh in a *perfect* way, he shall serve me;" which reads, "And the *perfect* shall remain in the land;" which reads, "The righteousness of the *perfect* shall direct his way;" which reads, "Let us, therefore, as many as be *perfect*;" which reads, "Every good *gift* and every *perfect gift* is from above," (as happiness, or "*blessedness?*"); which reads, "By works was faith made *perfect*;" which reads, "If any man offend not in word, the same is a *perfect* man" (a "*sinless*" man?); which reads, "Herein is our love made *perfect—perfect* love casteth out fear?" Yes, what of the Book that scores of times reads "*perfect?*" But such is the character of the *thing* we have for argument in this very critical controversy.

The Scottish version of this Psalm, tried by the final standard, and that standard in the hand of the able and honest scholar, will stand proudly *equal* with the prose; it is not ours here to say, *superior*. To scholars it can speak for itself. Controversial critics will run to the prose, and be of the same opinion still.

The *Sixteenth Psalm* is next most rudely assailed, and Rouse charged with gross doctrinal error and mistranslation. The charge here is a libel against God's word. It aims, not only at Rouse, but strikes at the prose and original text, too. It is laid on the *first* clause of the tenth verse, which in the prose reads thus, "For thou wilt not leave my *soul* in *hell*." The metrical version reads thus:

"Because my soul in *grave* to dwell, shall not be left by thee."

The whole weight of the vengeance of the critic turns upon one word differing from the *prose*. The latter renders *sheol*, "*hell;*" Rouse renders it "*grave;*" and on this difference he lays the following charges:

"(1.) That the *soul* goes down into the grave with the body. (2.) That the human soul of our blessed Lord was thus buried with his body. (3.) That 'his heart was glad' because his 'soul was not suffered to remain in the grave!'"

Now, such senseless jargon and libel against God's word betrays a bad cause and a worse advocate. For, by using the word *hell*, as in the prose, and approved by our critics, the conclusion will be as much more damaging to the Bible, as *hell* is a worse place for the *soul* than the *grave*. Will these horrible conclusions follow one whit the less from the rendering of the prose? Is it any better to send the *soul* with the body to *hell?* How much better can we expect from the spirit of the preface to these charges, and from the spirit that would approve of Watts' as the correct rendering? Hear our critics; thus they read:

"This is plainly the true sense—for how *could* David's *soul* (not his body) be left in the grave? Dr. Watts has given the correct rendering:

"'Though in the dust I lay my head,
  Yet, gracious God, thou wilt not leave
  My *soul* forever with *the dead*.'

"How much more accurate, theologically considered, is this than that of Rouse," says our critic.

What else, except a bad cause and worse advocate, must of necessity find David when Christ is in the Psalm? What else must find some phantasm of the *soul* of David, or somebody, going to *hell,* or going *"with the dead,"* instead of Christ's *body* going to the *grave?* And what else must put a pagan or popish construction upon the leading terms in the Psalm—as *Nephesh* and *sheol?* Had not the Holy Spirit settled the specific meaning of these words *as used here,* reckless controversialists might be excused in their shameful blundering. Acts iv. 31, excludes all verbal criticism, and closes all controversy about the verbal application of these terms. *The resurrection of Christ's body is the subject. Nephesh,* in the Psalm, means *Christ's body,* nothing else. It is oftened used of a *dead body,* a carcass. The following are some of the examples, as may be seen by turning to the Hebrew Bible—Lev. xxi. 1, 11; Lev. xxii. 4; Num. v. 2; Num. vi. 6; Num. xix. 11, 13; Num. ix. 6, 7, 10; Hag. ii. 13, *et al.* This *Nephesh, dead body* of Christ, went to the *grave,* the *"place of the dead"*—to the *sheol* of the Psalm. But Christ's *soul* never went to *sheol,* to the grave, to the place or *"state of the dead;"* nor to—worst and most shocking of all—*"hell!"* No, not for one moment. Christ's *soul* went immediately to paradise—to glory, the *place of the living.*

Sheol, here in this Psalm, by the *decision of the Holy Spirit* final, and from which there is no appeal, means the *grave* where Christ's *body* lay. Rouse translates it *grave,* which it means here, and nothing else. Our *prose* version renders it *hell,* which it don't mean here at all. Dr. Watts and the hymn-singers will have it, and sing it, neither *hell* nor the *grave;* but the *"dust,"* and *"with the dead,"* for they make both the *grave* and *purgatory* out of it; the one for the "*head*" (or body) of Christ; the other for the soul of Christ, thus—"My *head in the dust*"—"My *soul with the dead*," all from "*sheol*," and all "*the correct rendering* of Dr. Watts." About Watts' rendering we have here little to do, and care as little. The question with us is this: Is not our Scottish translation of *sheol* here *better* than the rendering of the prose? This is a matter neither of *debate* nor *verbal* criticism. The Spirit of God, in the Acts of the Apostles, puts this out of the way of special pleading; and to say that Rouse gives a better rendering here than the prose Bible, is but to use a simple *truism*. The champions who can write pages of this sort to condemn our Scottish version had as well not throw stones from the prose Bible, or from Watts' glasshouse. But stones must be thrown at our venerable metrical version, or the craft will be in danger. How much, for some desperate causes, can be made out of nothing! And, by-the-way, this hyper-criticism is a pretty fair specimen of the charges of mistranslations in our version of the Psalms.

The *Sixty-ninth Psalm* furnishes ground for the *third* charge of mistranslation and error. The last clause of the *fourth* verse in the prose reads thus, "Then I restored that which I took not away." This in the metre is rendered thus, "So what I took not, to render forced was I."

This rendering is charged with "very serious doctrinal and historical error;" and "to represent the atonement of Christ as compulsory;" to "overthrow the spiritual nature of the divine sacrifice; to misrepresent the inspired record, and contradict the Saviour himself." And "which of course utterly subverts the doctrine of atonement, by representing the blessed Saviour as a *forced victim* to divine justice! Still we have too much charity for these brethren to imagine they hold these *gross errors*." Very kind! We are not charged with the gross errors we sing! Ah, not much harm to sing gross error; since singing is like preaching, we can test by the Bible, take the good and reject the bad!

Believing candor to be a lovely trait in the character of a controversialist, we state freely that we shall not defend the word "forced" as the best possible turn of the English language by which to translate the original here. We confess to the defect in both our prose Bible and our Scottish version. And, further, we confess there are many instances in which both these versions fail to select the best possible words in the language; and yet they are, on the whole, both good translations, and both the word of God, just as all other fair translations of the scriptures are the word of God. In regard to the prose and metrical versions of this clause of the Psalm under consideration we remark:—

First. According to the rule of our learned critics, the prose is very defective; because it transposes the order of the original, the metre preserves it. *Second.* The prose fails to preserve the *causative* sense of the Hebrew verb, which is in the *Hiphil* or *causative* form. *Third.* The first verb, *Gezel*, is not fully rendered in either of the versions. It means to rob; to take by force or violence. It is too feebly rendered by, "*took not away;*" and therefore the antithesis of the original is lost in the rendering of the second verb. The first, meaning to take by force, and the second, being in the causative form, requires the antithetic form in rendering the second. While *forced* is liable to criticism, our translators might have used *caused* with safety.

Two forms of test may be applied here—theological and philological.

Theologically, two aspects favor our version; rendering, substantially—*First.* Christ's persecutors and murderers treated him as if he had been a robber, *making* him restore, as if he had by robbery appropriated what did not belong to him, and so was *forced* to render what he did not *rob*. *Second.* Christ voluntarily bound himself in covenant to restore what he took not away from the law. He was, therefore, made under the law. He was made sin for us. The law recognized him as our surety, and held him bound for the payment of our debt. Hence he says, "*Ought* not Christ to have suffered these things?" It was not possible the cup should pass from him. "Jehovah hath *made* to light on him the iniquity of us all. It was *exacted*, and he was *made* answerable." Isa. liii. 6, 7.

Philologically the metrical version is substantially vindicated. Versions have to do with the meaning of words. These we have noticed in part. But, further, the verb *Ashib*, in the future Hiphil, together with the antithesis with the context, warrant the rendering in the *causative* form. With this standard authorities agree. Luther renders thus, "Ich muss bezahlen, das ich nicht geraubet habe;" that is, "I *must* repay what I did not *rob*." Here the idea of the Scottish version is actually embodied and distinctly.

Dr. Alexander renders these words thus: "What I did not *rob*, then *must* I restore." Is this not *substantially* sustaining Rouse? We say *substantially*, for we concede the term *forced* is unhappily chosen, though *substantially* a literal rendering. It is strong and harsh. But is it not, to all competent and candid minds, as literal as the prose, and as really a version? If not, what shall we say of Luther, Alexander, and other scholars — indeed, of all scholars, for all must render *substantially* the same way?

We have now noticed the *three*, and the *only* instances in which our shrewd critics have discovered mistranslation and gross error in our metrical version. If more were to be found, more no doubt would have been found, and spread out over the emblazoned page. To the candid and ripe scholar, acquainted with scripture translations, the following will at once be his decision in regard to the translations in the *three* instances under consideration. They are, in both the English and Scottish versions, substantially fair translations; and in nothing does either of them, in anything essential, misrepresent the sense of the original. Thus vanishes the bitter gall, in the form of malignant charges of mistranslation and *gross error* in essential evangelical doctrine, into thin air. What a dust and smoke of malignant slander raised around a mere shade of error in translating *three* or *four* Hebrew words—*Ashre, Nephesh, Sheol, Ashib!* And then, *one* of these words translated into the very word used by our prose translators; and the only one of the four actually mistranslated in Rouse— *Nephesh* mistranslated *soul*—of course not noticed by our critics, because so found in their Test-Rule. *Another, sheol*, actually settled in its meaning in the Sixteenth Psalm by a rule ruling the rule of our friends, the Holy Spirit in Acts—ruling the correctness of the rendering in Rouse, the "*grave*." From this decision in favor of Rouse, the defendant, the critics have no appeal. In the *other two*, the Hebrew text being the rule, ruling all rules, and the judgment of the most erudite philologists applying that rule, is not the difference substantially in favor of defendant? Is not the Scottish version in the cases under consideration on the whole better than the prose? If the plaintiff has so signally failed here, in the strongest points possible for him to make, should he not suffer *non-suit*, pay damage and costs?

And now, after all the parade of words, sharp and bitter, poured out upon our Scottish version, its enemies have exhausted their magazines of wrath in windy charges against these *two* or *three* words as the only specimens of *gross error* and mistranslation. Can our prose version, after passing through such an ordeal of fire, maintain such a record?—only a word or two palpably *mis*translated from beginning to end? All other charges on which Rouse is condemned as patchwork—no version at all—belong to expletions, amplifications, etc. To these we shall attend in order. We now turn the tables.

AUDI ALTERAM PARTEM.

The very unpleasant work of comparing defects in translations is now before us. We again protest against this whole business, and again state that we suffer ourselves to be drawn into it only on necessary defence of truth, and as the last resort to arrest persistent warfare upon a version of a part of God's word which we hold dear.

MISTRANSLATIONS IN THE PROSE BIBLE USED BY THE FRIENDS OF UNINSPIRED PSALMODY AS THEIR TEST-RULE.

We here refer to the *first* class of errors in translation, to the *gross* and palpable kind, where a word is rendered by one of a different or opposite meaning, giving some other meaning aside the true one.

The word *Pneuma*, meaning spirit, is found in the New Testament about 400 times. In 222 instances it is applied to the Third Person of the Trinity. In some 132 times translated accurately *spirit*. In some 90 instances grossly mistranslated "*ghost.*"

Now God is a Spirit. But neither an *apparition*, a *wraith*, a *swarth*, a swairth, a *ghast*, a giest, nor a *ghost*. This is a damaging mistranslation, and has done immense damaging work to the doctrine of the Trinity, and to the Supreme Deity of the Holy Spirit. Thousands of our youth have had their minds poisoned by this mistranslation.

Thousands of shrewd Arians can scoff and cast in our teeth the stinging challenge—How can an apparition, a wraith, a ghost be God? All the mistranslations of Rouse put together will not equal these *ninety* cases of vital importance. Shall we stop here?

In Job xxvi. 7, we read: "Hangeth the earth upon nothing." The Hebrew, *balima*, is mistranslated "*nothing.*" It is found in Ps. xxxii. 9, translated "*bit and bridle.*" In Job it means "*restrainers,*" and doubtless refers to the *centrifugal* and *centripetal* forces holding the earth in its orbit.

In Ps. xliv. 2, the prose reads, last clause, "And cast them out," referring to the heathen, and is a mistranslation of the Hebrew "*tashalahim.*" This refers to "our fathers," and should read, "extend them," or increase them; as also Ps. lxxx. 11, "Spread out" as branches. See Dr. Alexander; also Scottish version.

In Ps. xvi. 10, we have a palpable instance in mistranslating *Nephesh* and *Sheol, soul*, and *hell*, both in violation of the analogy of faith in the text and elsewhere, settling the meaning in the Psalm to be *body* and *grave*, and nothing else.

The prose mistranslates Ps. lxii. 3, reading thus: "Ye shall be slain all of you; as a bowing wall *shall ye be, and as a* tottering fence." This reading makes the reference to enemies. The true rendering changes the reference to the speaker, thus: "Will ye murder all of you, like a wall inclined, a fence crushed?" That is, murder a man already crushed?

The prose mistranslates and changes the meaning of Ps. xcii. 11, reading thus: "Mine eye also shall see *my desire* on mine enemies, and mine ears shall hear *my desire.*" Literally thus: "Mine eye has looked upon my enemies—my ear shall hear." Simply, sees what becomes of enemies, not the gratification of desires on them. The same mistranslation is repeatedly found, as in Ps. liv. 7; Ps. lix. 10; Ps. cxii. 8; Ps. cxviii. 7, etc.

In Jerem. ii. 14, the following mistranslation occurs: "Home-born *slave*," where there is nothing like slave. The Hebrew is, "*Ilid baith,*" meaning "*son of my house.*"

In Luke xiv. 10, we read: "Then shalt thou have *worship.*" *Doxa* is found in the New Testament about 175 times, and when applied to man never means *worship*; this belongs to God alone.

We read in Acts xii. 4, thus: "Intending after *Easter.*" There is not a word in all the New Testament meaning *Easter* or Easter-day. That *day* belongs to *episcopacy*, not the word of God. *Pascha*, the Greek word, here means *Passover*, never Easter. In all Rouse there is not such a *gross* mistranslation.

In 1 John ii. 23, we read as follows: ("*But*) *he that acknowledgeth the Son hath the Father also.*" These words are in *Italics*, by which we are told that there is nothing for them in the text; but, being *understood*, the translators supply the ellipsis. If these words are in the original, to tell us, as our translators here tell us, they are not, is palpably to mistranslate. If they are not in the original, that is quite another matter—only a large patch asserting some considerable doctrinal teaching. Such would materially damage Rouse's divinity!

In 2 Cor. viii. 1, have we a translation of "*Gnoridzomen de humin,*" in these words: "Moreover, we do you, to wit?" Or is this a translation in English?—*We make known to you.*

In 1 Tim. i. 9, we read: "The law is not made for a righteous man." Is this true of the text, either *theologically* or *philologically?* The text is: "*Nomos ou keitai,*" meaning the law *lies not against*. The law is made for the rule of the righteous man's life; but its penalty lies not against him, but against the unrighteous man.

In Rev. xviii. 13, the word "*somaton*," meaning bodies, is rendered "*slaves.*"

In Lev. xxv. 44, and elsewhere, we have the mistranslation of the words, "*abed* and *amath*," by bondmen and bondmaids, when the meaning is simply servants, not slaves, as the translators meant. King James' translators were pro-episcopacy and pro-slavery, else why "*Easter*" and "*slave?*"

In reviewing all the *gross* mistranslations charged upon our Scottish version we find, upon actual and candid examination, only a single word or two, while many the most glaring are actually found in our prose Bible. In glancing over but a limited portion of our common Bible we find actually over one hundred *gross* mistranslations, for which there can be no apology or clearing explanation. We believe we can find hundreds more of the same class, many perhaps not so *gross*, but yet mistranslations. We have not been comparing King James' Bible with the Bishops', nor with any other translation, not even the Septuagint or Vulgate. Tyros and tricksters, conscious of a bad cause, may resort to such comparisons. In this way we have had Rouse exposed to invidious gaze *ad nauseam*. Had the enemies of a scripture psalmody been content with *truth* and the exposure of *facts*, had they kindly pointed out to us the expansions and amplifications that may mar and weaken our translation, and had they tested these by the true standard, we should certainly have thanked them. Such fraternal smiting would have been an oil to our heads. But, no, our friends, with an erring standard, imperfect like our own version, pronounce upon its imperfections. And, not content with this farce and insulting mockery, they add grim caricature and smarting misrepresentation. Of these by-and-by.

Before passing to another feature in the comparison of versions, we may notice what will be familiar to every scholar. The strong, sententious language and idiom of the Hebrew make it difficult to bring out into an English translation its great fulness and strength without apparent circumlocution. And, when the translation is in measured verse, the difficulty is enhanced. In translation, whether is the error greater to palpably misconstrue words of the Holy Spirit, giving for translation words of different or opposite meaning; or, to expand by a little circumlocution, while the meaning is retained and the analogy of faith is preserved inviolate? Translators should endeavor to avoid all unnecessary expansions; yet, since these blemishes will be found, so long as erring men translate, are we therefore to tell the heathen that the Bible, in the hundreds of languages in which we are sending it, is nothing more than a patchwork paraphrase, and not the veritable inspired word of God at all? Are we ready for that? Paganism, Islamism, Popery, Infidelity, will all, with ecstasy of joy, hail this concession. Christ did not so treat a translation inferior to both our English Bible and our Scottish version of the Book of Psalms. Though our Bible, as a translation, may have its blemishes, yet we are not willing therefore that the "*supreme judicatory*" should "*propose*" and "*sanction*" a body of divinity or a commentary "suited to the circumstances," and authorize its use instead of the Bible. Nor for any similar reasons are we willing that our Psalter should yield to any similar substitute.

"ROUSE'S PATCHWORK PARAPHRASE."

In replying to the charge of "*patchwork*" drawn out in masterly tactician form against Rouse, we wish to notice, *first*, some of the violations of the rules of honorable controversy. Honorable men, in honorable controversy, will state with truth and candor the positions of an opponent. In giving specimens of "*patchwork*," our friends should not *make for us* patches of *whole cloth*, and then tag them to our old coat, once of noble texture, warp and woof, long worn by our fathers, because now perhaps a little threadbare, or its cut a little out of fashion.

MANUFACTURED PATCHES CHARGED TO ROUSE.

In our prose Bible, Ps. lx. 6, reads thus: "God hath spoken in his holiness; I will rejoice." Alexander reads thus: "God hath spoken in his holiness; I will triumph." Rouse reads thus: "God in his holiness hath said; herein I will take pleasure." Each of these is a fair translation, without patch or paraphrase. Yet our friends, in their peculiar way, make and exhibit visible patchwork in opposite columns, thus:

PROSE VERSION.	ROUSE.
"God hath spoken in his holiness."	"God in his holiness hath said; *Herein I will take pleasure.*"

Here they leave out, in quoting the prose, what corresponds to the second line of Rouse in *italics*, and so change the entire line, a patch of their own make, while there is not the shadow of either patch or mistranslation, beside their own fabrication of whole cloth. Were this the only case of the kind we would pass it as a *lapsus*. But no. Again, we give the following verse entire; then the "*patch*" exhibit; Ps. lxvi. 6:

PROSE.	ROUSE.
"He turned the sea into dry land; they went through the flood on foot; there did we rejoice in him."	"Into dry land the sea he turned, And they a passage had; Ev'n marching through the flood on foot, There we in him were glad."

Now, the patch exhibit:—

"And they a passage had,
Ev'n marching through the flood on foot."

This second line is marked in *italics* to brand it as a patch, for which there is nothing in the original! Is there either *truth* or *candor* in this exhibit?

In Ps. xxxii. 6, we have another startling exhibit. To see it the better we give *three* translations of the clause:—

PROSE.	ALEXANDER.
"Surely in the floods of great waters they shall not come nigh unto him."	"Surely at the overflow of many waters, Unto him they shall not reach."

ROUSE.
"Surely, when floods of waters great do swell up to the brim,
They shall not overwhelm his soul, nor once come near to him."

Now see the exhibit, which truly sets Rouse in a ludicrous light, thus:—

"Surely when floods of waters great
Do swell up to the brim,
They shall not overwhelm his soul,
Nor once come near to him."

Here the *first* and *fourth* lines are presumed to be from the original; the middle lines patches. How, then, will the original read without the patches?—the pure original? Let us see:—

"Surely when floods of waters great
. . . .
. . . .
Nor once come near to him."

Take Ps. lxxviii. 33—writing Rouse, leaving *italics* in blank—we shall see how the original is made to read:—

"Wherefore their days in vanity He did consume, . . .
And . . . . their . . . in trouble . . ."

In Ps. lxxxiv. 12, they exhibit, by leaving out the *italics*, thus:—

"Who by . . . . on thee alone doth rest."

This represented as the text, or rule by which *Rouse* is

condemned as a patchwork, suggests on the face of it something omitted for effect. But supplying, as we have in the metrical version, we have just what the Hebrew warrants—"*assured confidence.*" So "*Baithhe*" means—as to *hang close, cling fast to*, etc., and is expressive of full assurance. But Rouse uses two words of many syllables—"rest by assured confidence," for trust in God. Now, if long words make patches, we had better, in translating, use monosyllables. Are there no polysyllables in the prose version?

These examples are only specimens of skill in garbling, misquoting, mis-italicizing Rouse, the better to make out a case. When these manufactured changes are deducted, and then the misconstructions and exaggerations, the patches will dwindle into proportions common to all faithful translations, our prose version not excepted.

MISCONSTRUCTIONS TO EXHIBIT PATCHES.

. We mean by misconstruction, the charging upon *Rouse*, as damaging *patchwork*, blemishes common to both versions. If expletives, in the form of qualifying words, or adjectives, etc., are found frequently in prose, as they are, and these destroy not its claim to our recognition as the word of God, why deny the same justice to the metrical version? This we think is both plain and fair

Examples.

PROSE VERSION.	ROUSE.
Ps. cii. 6. "I am like a pelican of the wilderness."	"Like pelican in wilderness, *Forsaken I have been.*"

We wish this to be carefully noticed, as an example illustrating principles here. The second line is set down as a large and damaging patch of "human composition," and so *italicized*. Now notice—the first line fails to make sense, the *verb* of the sentence is left out, consigned to *italics*. Perhaps, because, put in the preterite tense, "*I have been*," of the metre, is as agreeable to the Hebrews as "I am" of the prose. Then in all fairness our friend should have written us thus—"I have been like a pelican in the wilderness." This leaves the patch, really and honestly, very small, only the qualifying word, "*forsaken.*" But the pelican is a bird of *solitude*, and its use here is to suggest the idea of *loneliness* in the text. If such idea be in the text, and if, in composition similar, similar qualifying expletives are frequently found in the prose, as we shall show, then the damaging patch disappears.

The succeeding clause furnishes an illustration of the same principle:

"I am like an owl of the desert."   I am like the hooting night-bird of the desert.

Another class of Examples.

"I delayed not."   "I did not stay, *nor linger long, As those that slothful are.*"

The Hebrew word here is difficult to render fully without circumlocution. We believe it is never found in Kal; but in most instances, as here in the Psalm, in the *Hithpael*. As a participle here, with its reflective signification, it may be rendered:—I did not stand to ask questions, *how, what?* I did not stand still-I—shall-I? or dilly, dally. Harder to express than conceive the idea. In such construction expletives are not uncommon. Nor does Rouse vary materially from the very meaning of the text.

Another of the class.

"I thought on my ways."   "I thought upon my *former* ways, *And did my life well try.*"

It will be noticed here, as elsewhere, our friends in using their *italics* rigidly apply the prose version as the rule.

Were they to apply the original, often the result would be materially changed.

The Hebrew, *Hashab*, means more than the prose expresses. It means to add—superadd. Applied to thoughts, it means reflection—meditating over the past—and is copiously expressed in the amplified terms of our version. What thought beyond the spirit of the text is added?

It is not necessary that we vindicate every challenged expletive; nor is it essential that every one can be vindicated. No translation can claim such perfection. We claim no such perfection for our version. Nor can any man vindicate the mistranslations, or the burdensome and unnecessary expletives of our Bible.

SPECIMEN EXPLETIVES FROM OUR COMMON BIBLE.

John viii. 6. "But Jesus stooped down, and with *his* finger wrote on the ground, *as though he heard them not.*" Here is a patch large enough to harm Rouse very materially, if in the hands of our friends. Do the words of the sentence in the original suggest the idea of Christ's voluntary deafness, as loneliness is implied in the Psalm above? If these six words were not here, would we, in reading the words not marked in *italics*, naturally and undoubtedly entertain the idea that Christ did not hear, or that he was pretending not to hear? Is it not, at least, doubtful? But in the Psalm, can any one thoughtfully read the sentence without the word *forsaken*, and the question not occur—*how* like the pelican? Or without the idea of loneliness occurring to the mind? Still, if all this be denied, on what principle can we condemn the one and justify the other?

Acts xxviii. 4. "And when the barbarians saw the *venomous* beast hang." Here is a qualifying word suggested from the nature of the subject, though not in the original, and not in the least needed to make sense; and was fault ever found with it, as with scores of the kind in the Bible?

Rom. vii. 10. "And the commandment which *was ordained* to life, I found *to be* unto death." Here are two verbs added; one expressive of action not implied in the original, viz: *was ordained.* Or, if implied, as suggested by the text, certainly with evidence no clearer than, "forsaken," in the Psalm above. And then why not render the sentence thus: "And the commandment for life, I found for death?" In all such cases in Bible and in Psalm, let both go unchallenged together.

Rom. xi. 16. "If the first fruit *be* holy, the lump *is* also *holy.*" We notice this not only for an offset to this class of patches now under consideration, but to meet the charge of adding "*adjectives*" and qualifying words. Hundreds of such are in the prose Bible. Of course we can stay to give a few specimens only.

1 Cor. 14. "*Unknown,*" is used *five* times to qualify *tongue*; and *six* times omitted where the word *tongue* is used.

1 Pet. iii. 2. "Behold your chaste conversation *coupled* with fear." In this construction of the sentence, *coupled* is a comment settling what seems to be assumed as uncertain. Why not read without the supplement thus: "Beholding in reverence your chaste conversation?"

2 Pet. ii. 18. "They allure through the lusts of the flesh, *through much* wantonness." Here are qualifying words not in the original, of doubtful character. They burden the sense, and change the degree of the attribute or quality of the subject of the affirmation. Such expletives would be large explanation in Rouse, and a damaging *patch.* But certainly right in the Test-Rule.

2 Pet. iii. 1. "This second epistle, beloved, I now write unto you; in *both* which—" I refer to this not because

the italicised word, "*both*," should not be inserted, but because we have here a good subject to illustrate the unfairness of the rule by which our brethren test our version. If we look not behind the English in our translation here, we may justly condemn the use of the qualifying word "*both*." Because, the question, whether Peter includes the *first* with the *second* epistle, or "*this*," the second only, cannot be settled without reference to the original. Here the relative "*which*" being plural requires *both*, if ellipsis be supplied. Must all patches in Rouse of this kind, because differing from the prose, be condemned as cancelling its claim to recognition as a version?

Jude 8. "Also these *filthy* dreamers defile the flesh." Just such use of qualifying is sweepingly condemned in Rouse. How do we know whether these dreamers were *filthy* or chaste *dreamers*, good or bad, true or false, visionary or real? Is *filthy* a divine or human word? Inspired or uninspired? How is this, and all such cases? For just so we are taunted in page after page, and paragraph after paragraph. Is this kind of thing fair?

Job xii. 6. "Into whose hand God bringeth *abundantly*." To add the qualifying word here is adding to the sense, and materially changes the meaning. This would be a human patch in Rouse, and would spoil his divinity. How with Job? Our friends should be posted here in adjusting scales and grading rules.

Amos iv. 3. "And ye shall go out at the breaches, every *cow at that which is* before her."

How shall we justify the addition to the original of these words in *italics?* Not a word in the verse or sentence about cows. We have to travel back ten lines before we find "kine" in the context. If our brethren will justify the patching here, it will aid in answering many of their objections, and help to chasten their Christian style of treating the Book of Psalms.

Exodus xii. 36. "And the Lord gave the people favor in the sight of the Egyptians, so that they lent unto them *such things as they required.*" Are our friends sure these words in *italics* are not human?

Numbers xiv. 27. "How long *shall I bear with* this evil congregation, which murmur against me?" Why not read thus: How long this evil congregation murmuring against me? Rather different reading.

2 Sam. xx. 19. "I *am of them that are* peaceable." "I peaceable" is inspired; are the other six words?

1 Kings xx. 12. "Set *yourselves in array*. And they set *themselves in array* against the city." Set, and they set against the city. A military order—form—and they formed against the city.

2 Kings x. 24. "If any of the men whom I have brought into your hands escape, *he that letteth him go* his life *shall be* for the life of him." Are these words: "*he that letteth him go, shall be,*" inspired?

1 Chron. xix. 18. "Seven thousand men *which fought in* chariots." Why not: "Seven thousand charioteers?"

1 Chron. xxviii. 21. "Behold, the courses of the priests and the Levites, *even they shall be with thee* for all the service of the house of God; and *there shall be* with thee, for all manner of workmanship." May we not read thus: "Behold, the courses of the priests and the Levites with thee for all the service of the house of God, and for all manner of workmanship?" Any human patches here? Only *nine* or ten words.

Job xxxiv. 10. "Far be it from God *that he should do* wickedness, and *from* the Almighty *that he should commit* iniquity." Could not the *italics* be omitted here, and the strength of the sense increased? Thus: "Wickedness is far from God, iniquity from the Almighty." Forty-six letters inspired, forty-six uninspired. How is this?

Again, verses 17-19. "Wilt thou condemn him that is most just? *Is it fit* to say to a king, *thou art* wicked? *and* to princes, *ye are* ungodly? *How much less to him* that accepteth not the persons of princes."

Read the "patches" grouped together—*Is it fit, thou art, and, ye are, How much less to him?*"

Now read the inspired words: "Wilt thou condemn him that is most just, saying to a king, wicked? to princes, ungodly? accepting not the persons of princes?"

Reader, patience a moment. Remember, our friends charge on our version explanations, additions, repetitions, human compositions; and conclude, therefore, Rouse is "no version at all." We wish to show that they prove too much—proving our version, no version, they prove the Bible no version.

CONDENSED, PROMISCUOUS GROUPING EXAMPLES FOR ILLUSTRATION.

"For they considered not *the miracle of* the loaves." "For they considered not the loaves." "*The miracle*" is an explanation, is comment, not translation, strictly.

"Is not mine to give, but *it shall be given to them* for whom *it is* prepared." Text: "Is not mine to give, but for whom prepared." This occurs in several instances, and always unnecessarily.

"Two *women shall be* grinding at the mill." Text: "Two grinding at the mill."

"Ye know that after two days is *the feast of* the passover." "After two days is the passover." This occurs again and again in the New Testament, only burdening the force of the expression.

"A *certain* man planted a vineyard, and set a hedge

around it, and digged *a place for* the winefat." Text: "A man planted a vineyard, hedged and digged a winefat."

"For ye know not when the time is; *for the Son of man is* as a man taking a far journey." Text: "For, as a man taking a far journey, ye know not when the time is." Is there not here, *first*, a useless addition; and *second*, an improper use of "*The sacred Name?*"

In Luke iii. 23–38, we have seventy-five repetitions of two words, making 150 words in fifteen verses, without corresponding words in the original, and adding no strength to the meaning.

"But *this cometh to pass* that the word might be fulfilled." Text: "But that the word might be fulfilled."

"Because their country was nourished by the king's *country*." Why not by the king's "*bounty?*"

"Especially *because I know* thee to be expert." Why not thus: "Since thou art expert?"

"Therefore, as by the offence of one *judgment came* upon all men to condemnation; even so by the righteousness of one, *the free gift came* upon all men." Here is addition upon addition, darkening rather than explaining. This is the simple statement: "As through one offence—so through one righteousness."

"Because *they sought it* not by faith." Text: "Because not by faith."

"Who have not bowed the knee to *the image of* Baal." Text: "Who have not bowed the knee to Baal."

"My brethren, by them *which are of the house* of Chloe." Text: "My brethren, by them of Chloe."

"Who maketh thee to differ *from another?*" Text: "Who distinguish thee?"

"A dispensation *of the gospel* is committed unto me." Text: "I am intrusted with a stewardship."

"It is not permitted unto them to speak; but *they are*

commanded to be under obedience." Text: "It is not permitted unto them to speak, but to be under obedience." This patch is pretty broad and *stern*.

"For *one* star differeth from *another* star in glory." Better: "Star differeth from star in glory." This specimen of slight addition, apparently trifling, yet, to any competent scholar, it clearly weakens the text, and mars its sublimity and euphony. Even secular journals are noticing these things, and suggesting the importance of a general revision of the whole Bible. Another instance of apparently trifling use of ellipsis, yet materially affecting the sense :—

"The last *enemy* that shall be destroyed *is* death." Is not the averment here the *order* of destruction?—death the *last* enemy to be destroyed? Whereas, is not this the affirmation of the *text:* "Death, the last enemy, shall be destroyed?" Is not the office, and effect of these expletives obviously comment?

"But now much more diligent, upon the great confidence which *I have* in you. Whether *any do inquire* of Titus, *he is* my partner and fellow-helper concerning you; or our brethren *be inquired of, they are* the messengers of the churches." Text: "Upon the great confidence in you, or of Titus, my partner and fellow-helper, concerning you; or our brethren, the messengers of the churches."

"The law was our schoolmaster *to bring us* unto Christ." Or, "Our schoolmaster unto Christ."

"For *that day shall not come.*" Text: "For."

This last specimen looks so much like the examples of our friends, we place in juxta-position the following—*par nobile!* :—

PROSE VERSION.	ROUSE.
"I delayed not."	"I did not stay, *nor linger long, As those that slothful are.*"

" Neither give heed to... which minister questions, rather than godly edifying, which is in faith; *so do.*" Do what? Paul dissuades Timothy in the text. And this patch breaks the connection with the verse following :—

"Forbidding to marry, *and commanding* to abstain from meats." Text: "Forbidding to marry, and to use meats."

"*I pray God* that it may not be laid to their charge." Text: "May it not be laid to their charge." Is this "patch" needed here to supply anything? And, then, does this profane the Divine name, as charged upon our version?

"And not for ours only, but also for *the sins of* the whole world." Text: "And not for ours only, but also for the whole world." Is this not comment, unnecessarily impinging upon a theological controversy?

"And *I will write upon him* my new name." Text: "And my new name." Is this repetition?

We have selected from a part of our English Bible a few specimens only out of hundreds upon hundreds found in the Test-Rule of our brethren. Space and our readers' patience forbid extension.

One *class* more of charges requires attention :

THE USE OF THE DIVINE NAMES AND ATTRIBUTES.

Everything that can excite prejudice against our Scottish version of the Psalms has been ingeniously paraded and emblazoned on the pages of controversy, and spread out before the gaze of the public eye. And all this for partisan effect, as ungenerous as injurious. It is distinctly insinuated that Rouse is guilty of profaning the Divine name by its use when it is not found in the original. We are challenged thus: "Can this be a sacred use of these awful TITLES of the Sovereign of all worlds?"

We admit that in some instances the charge against Rouse is, at least, worthy of consideration. If there were no such instances in the prose Bible we should, perhaps feel startled at the bold charge. I presume here, as else where, our friends did not think of this when hurling stones at Rouse. Had the facts been before their minds it is pre sumed that, as skilled controversialists, they would have written with more modesty and Christian charity. In many instances, where the translators of our Bible use the Divine name, no principle or rule of translating requires such licence. We are not prepared to vindicate or censure. The right or wrong here is for our brethren to settle. Indeed, this should have been done before committing themselves to the condemnation of their standard by which they condemn us. Were this thing wrong, and our common Bible innocent, we should make concessions.

We have hastily run our eye over several books of the Bible, and have noticed about eighty instances of the use of the Divine name where it is wanting in the original. It is probable there are more than *one hundred* instances in the entire Bible. Nor are we prepared to say that there is a single instance in which the Divine name might not be omitted without prejudice to the sense, either by the use of the pronoun, or by changing the structure of the sentence.

SPECIMENS OF TRANSLATORS' USE OF THE DIVINE NAME WHERE WANTING IN THE ORIGINAL.

Deut. xvi. 10: "And thou shalt keep the feast of weeks unto the Lord thy God with a tribute of a free-will offering of thine hand, which thou shalt give *unto the* LORD *thy God*, according as the Lord thy God hath blessed thee." The omission could not impair the sense here.

Deut. xxxiii. 12: "The beloved of the Lord shall dwell in safety by him; *and the Lord* shall cover him all the day long."

2 Chron. iii. 1: "Then Solomon began to build the house

of the Lord at Jerusalem in Mount Moriah, where *the Lord* appeared unto David." Why not the pronoun here?

2 Chron. xvii. 4: "But sought to the *Lord* God of his father." Superfluous here.

Neh. vi. 9: "Now, therefore, *O God*, strengthen my hands." Similar to many Psalms.

Isa. xxvi. 1: "Salvation will *God* appoint for walls and bulwarks." This being song is similar, in its use of the Divine name, to many of the cases occurring in the Psalms.

Acts vii. 59: "And they stoned Stephen calling upon *God*, and saying, Lord Jesus receive my spirit." Evidently unnecessary here. A different construction will make the name superfluous.

1 Cor. xvi. 2: "Let every one of you lay by him in store, as *God* hath prospered him."

Rom. ix. 4: "To whom *pertaineth* the adoption, and the glory, and the covenants, and the giving of the law, and the service of *God*, and the promises." McKnight reads: "And the worship, and the promises."

James ii. 1: "Have not the faith of our Lord Jesus Christ, *the Lord* of glory." This can be avoided by otherwise constructing the sentence.

2 Tim. iv. 16: "*I pray God* that it may not be laid to their charge." There can be no plea for the use of the Divine name more than in any Psalm where it is used. The meaning is simply: "Let it not be laid to their charge."

Heb. ix. 6: "The priests went always into the first tabernacle, accomplishing the service *of God*." Here the service of the tabernacle is the reference, and the Divine name superfluous.

Col. i. 19: "For it pleased *the Father* that in him should all fulness dwell." The insertion here is not only superfluous, but raises a theological question that belongs to exposition, not to translation.

1 Thess. v. 23: "And the very God of peace sanctify you wholly; and *I pray God* your whole spirit and soul and body be preserved."

In Ps. xxiv. 6, the Septuagint supplies the Divine name: "*God* of Jacob." And our prose Bible supplies *twice* in Ps. cxxxii. 2 and 5: "Mighty *God* of Jacob."

Gen. xliv. 7: "*God forbid* that thy servants should do according to this thing." And verse 17: "And he said: *God forbid* that I should do so." The Hebrew word *Halile* is so translated in the Old Testament some eight or ten times, where there is no more need for using the Divine name than in the instances charged against Rouse. "*Far be it,*" or some such equivalent, would as faithfully translate the original as, "*God forbid,*" and so escape the indirect charge, preferred by our friends, of profanely using the Divine name.

Luke xx. 16: "And when they heard it they said: "*God, forbid*"—"*Mee genoito.*"

Rom. iii. 4, 6, 31: "*God forbid;*" given as the rendering of the Greek, which simply means—"*By no means,*" and fully renders the original. See *McKnight.*

This misuse of the Divine name occurs some fifteen times in the New Testament; some twenty-three times at least in the Bible; beside the other forms, in all perhaps more than one hundred times. In many instances, similar to those where the Divine name is used, its insertion does not occur, which suggests a doubt in regard to the necessity of such rendering in any instance. And what is the more singular here, in these twenty-three instances, *italics* are not used, as in other cases where the reader is informed there is no corresponding word in the original.

We cannot extend quotations. Five or six times the number might have been added. Enough to show the *animus* of our extreme critics. It is presumed that where the Divine Being is the object or subject of a sentence, our translators have not scrupled to write the name. Perhaps they had not studied the subject as carefully as our pious friends of the hymn-book—perhaps not so tenderly scrupulous in their conscience. Under all the circumstances we shall leave this question of casuistry *sub judice,* hoping our friends will issue an exegetical thesis which will save us and all our translators from future blunders.

We would here, in the mean time, before parting with our friends, venture, in a fraternal and charitable spirit, to advise them to extend their acquaintance with their Bible. It will aid them in their warfare upon translations. It may save them from exposing their want of reasonable knowledge of subjects on which they can write with wonderful assurance and flippancy. It may greatly simplify their style, and save them from that most repulsive and characteristic *ex cathedra* feature of their polemic discussions of this favorite subject.

CHAPTER VI.

THE SCOTTISH VERSION COMPARED WITH THE SEPTUAGINT.

Why this comparison—Its importance in this discussion—The established opinion and decision of the Churches in regard to the Septuagint as a translation—Its defects compared with those of the Scottish version—The claims of the Scottish version sustained by such comparison—Luther's translation incidentally noticed—Inferences.

THE claims of any particular version are not to be settled finally by comparison with any other received version. The original text is the only true test, and by this ours must stand or fall. Yet, on several accounts, it becomes essential to our discussion to compare the Scottish version with others long received and acknowledged.

First, because our friends have made a received translation a test by which they have with extreme severity put our version on trial.

Second, because, if our version will compare favorably with other received versions, our friends are refuted on their own chosen ground, and our version is sustained triumphantly against unreasonable cavil.

Third, because, though this is *argumentum ad hominum*, yet it seems to be the only and last resort through which to meet our oppponents, and silence their unreasonable charges and appeals to popular prejudice and ignorance.

The Protestant churches, in this age of Bible translation and dissemination, are not prepared for the condemnation of any one version because not perfect, and because some blemish may be found not common to all other versions, since all versions are human, and each may have some peculiar defect of its own. Our point in this chapter is not how good our version may be; but has it, on comparison with others, a right to a fellowship among other recognized versions of the Scriptures?

There are four recognized translations, of long and established reputation, in four different languages. The Septuagint in the Greek, the Vulgate in the Latin, Luther's Bible in the German, and our own in the English. Opinions may differ in regard to their respective merits as versions. The Septuagint has enjoyed a longer and more universal recognition than any one of the others. The Jews, the Greek and Roman Catholics and Protestants, have appealed to the Greek Bible of the Seventy as the inspired word of God, as we appeal to our English Bible. A version that has been recognized by the whole Church for two thousand years can hardly be ignored as a patchwork or paraphrase for the sake of effect in controversy. If it be a translation, and yet more and grosser mistranslations are found in it than can be found in the Scottish version of the Psalms, then this is a translation. In a question of this kind the harmonious statements of standard and unchallenged authors should be received without challenge.

THE SEPTUAGINT.

We quote from the deservedly celebrated Prof. Gaussen, of Geneva, Switzerland, on the *Inspiration of the Bible*, pp. 161–163:—

"The sacred authors of the New Testament, when they themselves quote the old Hebrew Scriptures in Greek, employ for that purpose the *Greek translation,* so called of *the Seventy,* executed at Alexandria two centuries and a half before Jesus Christ.

"No more is required, in fact, than to study the manner in which the Apostles employ the Septuagint, in order to see in it a striking sign of the verbal inspiration under which they wrote.

"Although it was the universal practice of the Hellenistic Jews, throughout the whole East, to read in their synagogues and to quote in their discussions the Old Testament, according to that ancient version, the Apostles show us the independence of the spirit that guided them by the three several methods they follow in their quotations."

These quotations, if their accuracy be admitted, prove— *First*, that the Jews, two hundred and fifty years before Christ, used, in their synagogues, the Septuagint as the Scriptures in their vernacular tongue. *Second*, Christ and his Apostles found this Greek copy of the Scriptures in the synagogues of the Jews generally — always where they understood the Greek language. *Third*, the writers of the New Testament wrote in the same language, and quote from the Septuagint as from a generally recognized version.

We quote from *Smith's Bible Dictionary*, p. 507:—

"The Septuagint version was highly esteemed by the Hellenistic Jews before the coming of Christ. The manner in which it is quoted by the writers of the New Testament proves that it had been long in general use. Wherever, by the conquests of Alexander, or by colonization, the Greek language prevailed; wherever Jews were settled, and the attention of the neighboring Gentiles was drawn to their wondrous history and law, there was found the Septuagint, which thus became, by Divine Providence, the means of spreading widely the knowledge of the One True God, and his promises of a Saviour to come, throughout the nations. Not less wide was the influence of the Septuagint in the spread of the Gospel. The Ethiopian eunuch was reading the Septuagint version of Isaiah in his chariot. They who were scattered abroad went forth into many lands speaking of Christ in Greek, and pointing to the things written of Him in the Greek version of Moses and the Prophets."

Besides confirming Gaussen, this testimony shows how this translation went with the New Testament Scriptures in their diffusion wherever Christianity spread in the first Christian centuries; and so the whole Bible, Old and New Testaments, went together in the same language. No translation ever had a more universal recognition as the word of God in any age or in any country.

From Horne we make the following quotations, vol. i., pp. 264, etc. :—

"Among the Greek versions of the Old Testament, the *Alexandrian* or *Septuagint*, as it is generally termed, is the most ancient and valuable; and was held in so much esteem, both by the Jews and by the first Christians, as to be constantly read in the synagogues and churches. Hence it is uniformly cited by the early Fathers, whether Greek or Latin; and from this version all the translations into other languages which were anciently approved by the Christian Church were executed, except the Syriac.

"The Septuagint version gradually acquired the highest authority among the Jews of Palestine, who were acquainted with the Greek language, and subsequently also among Christians."

References to the same import might be greatly extended. The Septuagint has for two thousand years held a high and unquestioned authority as a translation. Notwithstanding, the current testimony makes equally clear that this translation has many defects—abounds in mistranslations.

How will it compare with the Scottish version?—This is our present inquiry. Horne says, p. 266:—

"The translator of the book of Job being acquainted with the Greek poets, his style is more elegant and studied; but he was not sufficiently master of the Hebrew language and literature, and consequently his version is very erroneous. Many of the historical passages are interpolated; and in the poetical parts there are several passages wanting. Jerome, in his preface to the book of Job, specifies as many as seventy or eighty. The Psalms and Prophets were translated by men every way unequal to the task."

Of Origin it is said: "When any passages appeared in the Septuagint that were not found in the Hebrew, he designated them by an *obelus*. And, in lieu of the very erroneous Septuagint version of Daniel, Theodotian's translation of that book was inserted entire."

Enough to show the universal reputation of the Septuagint—*first*, as an acknowledged translation of the books of the Old Testament; and *second*, as having many gross mistranslations, additions, omissions, interpolations, and explanations; and with all these defects, still never, even by the best scholars, denounced as "patchwork, paraphrase, no version at all." Such denunciation is left to controversial extravagance.

Horne gives a list of the quotations from the Old Testament in the New, in some of which we have specimens of the Septuagint's mistranslations. We shall give a few examples:—

PROSE VERSION.	SEPTUAGINT.
Mich. v. 2: "But thou, Bethlehem Ephratah, *though* thou be little among the thousands of Judah."	"But as for thee, Bethlehem, thou house of Ephratha, art thou the least (or too little to become one) of the thousands of Judah?"
Hos. xi. 1: "I ... called my son out of Egypt."	"I called his children out of Egypt."
Isa. xlii. 1: "Behold my servant, whom I uphold; mine elect, in whom my soul delighteth."	"Jacob is my servant, I will uphold him; Israel is my chosen, my soul hath embraced him."
Zech. xi. 13: "Cast it unto the potter; a goodly price that I was prized at of them."	"Put them into the smelting furnace, and I will see whether it is proof, in like manner as I have been proved by them."

PROSE VERSION.	SEPTUAGINT.
Zech. xii. 10: "They shall look on me whom they have pierced."	"They will look to me, instead of the things concerning which they have contemptuously danced."
Gen. xviii. 10: "I will certainly return unto thee according to the time of life."	"I will return to thee about this time twelvemonth."
Isa. viii. 14: "He shall be . . . for a stone of stumbling and a rock of offence to both the houses of Israel."	"And ye shall not run against a stumbling stone, nor as under a falling rock."
Prov. x. 12: "Love covereth all sins."	"But friendship covereth all them who are not contentious."

These are but a small specimen of a single class. We might add hundreds more, and in addition to the seventy or eighty verses omitted in Job. A few, in addition, from the book of Psalms:—

Ps. iv. 2: "How long . . . my glory into shame?"	"How long will ye be obstinate?" (*Barukardioi.*)
Ps. iv. 3: "But know that the Lord hath set apart him that is godly for himself."	"But know ye that the Lord has made wonderful his saint."
Ps. xvi. 3: "To the saints that are in the earth, and to the excellent, in whom is all my delight."	"To the saints in his earth, in them has he made wonderful all his will."
Ps. xxii. 1: "Why hast thou forsaken me . . . from the words of my roaring?"	Added: "*Give heed to me*"— words of my *transgressions*, for "roarings."
Ps. cx. 3: "Thy people shall be willing in the day of thy power, in the beauties of holiness from the womb of the morning: thou hast the dew of thy youth."	"With thee is the beginning in the day of thy power, in the splendors of thy saints. Out of the womb before the morning star I begot thee."

This brief exhibit presents a very limited view of even specimen defects in the translations of the Septuagint. Our time, space, the nature of the subject, and the patience of our readers, suggest cursory notice. We might here, in the same way, show the errors of Luther's translation. Subsequent translators and commentators have made this matter plain enough. Error in Luther's Bible is not, at this day, a matter of controversy. Nor is it a matter of question whether any translation is free from mistranslations. It may be a matter of question whether some of these recognized translations do not, in their mistranslations, surpass any error that can be found in our Scottish version.

In regard to the comparative merits of Luther's translation, Gaussen makes the following statement:—

"The version of an accomplished rationalist, who desires to be no more than a translator, I could better trust than that of an orthodox person and a saint, who should paraphrase the text, and undertake to present it to me more complete or more clear in his French than he found it in the Greek or in the Hebrew of the original. And let no one be surprised at this assertion; it is justified by facts. Thus, is not De Wette's translation, among the Germans, preferred at the present day to that even of the great Luther? At least is there not greater confidence felt in having the mind of the Holy Spirit in the lines of the Basel professor than in those of the great reformer; because the former has always kept very close to the expressions of the text, as a man of learning, subject to the rules of philology alone; while the latter seems at times to have momentarily endeavored after something more, and sought to make himself interpreter as well as translator?"

As Luther's Bible might be improved, so for the same reasons might our English Bible; and it should be, were the reliable instrumentalities available.. Our Psalter might be improved, and it should be. We know this and feel it. In the work of its improvement we are making some effort. And what do these acknowledged facts prove? One thing they do not prove, with all the blemishes found—they don't prove these versions to be "mere patchwork, paraphrase, no versions at all." De Wette's version may be, doubtless is, better than Luther's. Is, therefore, Luther's now, since the publication of De Wette's, no translation at all? Luther's Bible is still reputed a version of the Scriptures, the word of God, as other human translations are.

Should some sect, on the ground of some "patches" in our Bible, draw up a commentary, embracing its own creed faithfully, and "grouping" all "essential" truths of the Bible, and use it for all the purposes for which evangelical churches use the Scriptures; and should some church reprove for such use of a commentary and abuse of the word of God, and should it be retorted: "Three are mistranslations, errors doctrinal and historical, paraphrases, explanations, etc., in your Bible, and you use nothing better than our commentary, and then our commentary needs no explanation,"—would the friends of the Bible own they had no inspired Scriptures, and that they had been under delusion about translations and versions? Friends and brethren, on all sides of this controversy, we will venture to say for you all here, none of us are ready for any such conclusions. Nor are the friends of a scripture psalmody ready to abandon the use of our inspired songs because of the equally unjust charges made against our divine psalter.

If Luther's Bible, the Septuagint—saying nothing of hundreds of versions going to the heathen—and our own English version, have all their defects in translation, and yet are all recognized as versions of the Scriptures, how can we refuse the Scottish version, as free from mistranslation as any of them, a recognition to fellowship in the family of versions? How cast it off as a "human composition," and consign it to cold fellowship with Dr. Watts' imitations and hymns? Candor demands for it better company; for, if it be not the word of God inspired, then we have not the word of God inspired in the vernacular tongues.

Until our friends shall revolutionize the entire theory and practice of the Church for two thousand years on the subject of versions, we shall remain unmoved by all their refined amenity and Christian charity, so fraternally exhibited in their charges upon Rouse's "patchwork, paraphrase, no version at all, gross error in doctrine."

It is due to state here, by way of concession, that, while it is true that mistranslations and blemishes charged upon Rouse are all of their kind, more or less, found in our Bible and in the Septuagint, even to the violation of the order of the original, as in the case of the Septuagint changing the order of the commandments, yet it is just to admit that there are a few cases of poetic licence in which too much is added. These occur in the *second* versions mostly and in the particular metres, as in Psalms cxxiv., cxxxvi., and cxliii. Like hundreds of instances in our Bible and in the Septuagint, these should be reviewed and corrected. In this work we are as a church engaged, and, according to our ability, are endeavoring to make progress. We admit, what candor demands for every translation known, there are instances where correction should be made. We admit, further, the age and circumstances demand for the inspired Psalms a better dress, a higher literary and poetic finish. And it is to be hoped that these Psalms, now under process of correction and improvement, will, under a kind Providence, soon appear in an improved form in some measure equal to their merit.

Another consideration might be urged upon the friends of a Scripture psalmody. The singing, in too many of our churches, is every way inferior to the merit and claims of our inspired, soul-moving songs. The dulness of our music, and the indifference of so many of the friends of the Bible Psalms to the cultivation of congregational singing, give occasion to charge the defect upon the Psalms themselves. There is a life and power in the divinely inspired songs justifying the highest attainments in sacred vocal music.

CHAPTER VII.

CONCLUSION.

The argument from history—Very briefly noticed—Of comparatively little importance in this controversy—Yet some facts of history with consideration—The Palatinate Churches—History not the rule of faith and worship—The mistake and its fatal consequences—Appeal to our readers—Address to brethren in the ministry—Appeal to the friends of union.

WE do not here propose to enter upon any formal argument from history. It has its use and its place. It is neither legislator nor judge. It can settle nothing as a matter of faith, of practice, or of worship. God's word, revealed in the Scriptures, alone authorizes worship, with all its ways and forms. Anything not instituted in the word, as a way of worship, is not only without authority, but is sin forbidden, is violation of God's law.

The province of history is to settle the occurrence of, events, as their facts, their times, their places, their circumstances; but never what is truth, or right, or duty, or how God is to be worshipped.

Our opponents think they find much use for history in this controversy, and no doubt feel more at home here than in the Bible. They are not alone here. Presbyterianism finds more sturdy weapons drawn from history—from "*the Fathers*"—levelled against her, than all that can be wrested from the armory of God's word. Episcopacy, and even papacy, draw their keenest blades from the Fathers. Presbytery and its advocates are at home in the Scriptures. Just so in this controversy, we are not much concerned in regard to this section of the field. If we are able to show that argument from history can avail our brethren but little in their cause of uninspired hymns, this is enough for us. For, indeed, from the very nature of the case what *can* history prove? Then

WHAT IS THE SUM OF HISTORICAL EVIDENCE PROVING THE DIVINE RIGHT OF HYMN-MAKING?

What *writer* of hymns, or hymn-book, among all the authors of the first five centuries of the Christian era, has been carried down in history to our times? Why has not one single psalm, hymn, or spiritual song, composed within those five centuries, outlived the centuries, preserved its continuous use, its pristine, apostolic redolence, and found its way down intact to our times? Why, the *name* of not one single Christian poet who composed, or one single presbytery, synod, assembly, or council, that received, examined, amended, authorized to be sung in the worship of God, with the time, the place, or people among whom such making, adoption, and use occurred? Why, since in every century the names of so many Fathers—so many of their works on every topic of theology and matter of history—commentaries, homilies, theological disputations, defences, apologies, and even creeds, Apostles', Athanasian, etc., have all found their way down through the ages, leaving their distinct traces upon their annals, and yet neither poet nor hymnbook? From the days of Homer and Pindar, down through the times of Horace and Virgil, on till the days of Byron, every age and language produced its poets and its songs. The world abounds in the works of poets hundreds of years before Christ and since; but where the record of the poets, the hymns, and the hymn-books of the Church for centuries, till anti-Christian apostacy, corruption in worship invaded by ritualism the simplicity of divinely instituted worship, and made and authorized and used uninspired songs?

CONCLUSION. 159

Since papal hymn-singing and *Ave Marias* were introduced, since Lutheran Protestants have figured in history and as historians, since the extended use of uninspired denominational hymns among the large and popular churches, church records and church history abound with their allusions to poets, their hymns, and their hymn-books, as things with which the annalist is as familiar as with the Bible, with bible-making, bible use, bible knowledge, bible-quoting. Scarcely can any popular book be written upon any religious subject, from the ponderous quarto tome of the most learned commentator, down to the Sabbath-school primer, but stanzas and couplets from the favorite hymn-book must embellish almost every page or paragraph. If hymn-singing shall mark the character of the Church for a thousand years to come, can the name of Watts and Wesley, with their hymn-books and their hymns, pass away from the page of history and the memory of a hymn-singing Church? Who were the Watts and the Wesleys of the first five centuries of the Christian era? Who were the Watts and the Wesleys of the Waldensian Churches? Who made the hymns in the days and for the Churches of Calvin and Knox? Who made the hymns sung by the brave Huguenots under Henry of Navarre, when on their knees they prayed and sung in full chorus before smiting their enemies "hip and thigh?" Who made the hymns sung by the brave Republican Hollanders before joining in battle with the terrible legions of Philip? Even the historian of Henry of Navarre and William the Silent, Prince of Orange, can record the names of the poets of those times, their hymn-books, and their hymns, *alias Psalms*.

And just here, by-the-way, we have the clew to the secret of that apparently successful use of history on the part of our friends, who, like the friends of episcopacy, find themselves at home in history and among the Fathers. Our own Motley, writing of Henry of Navarre and the Huguenots, says:—

"'They went on their knees before the battle, and singing in full chorus a Psalm of David before smiting the Philistines hip and thigh."

He says, speaking of the siege of Valenciennes, "whose whole population nearly was of the Calvinistic faith:"—

"The music of Marot's sacred songs (a version of the Psalms) happened that morning to be sounding forth from every belfry the Twenty-second Psalm."

Motley tells us that "the Psalms were translated into Flemish verse for the use of the Reformed Churches by Philip de Marnix." Afterward he styles this same Marnix "the poet, the orator, and *hymn-book maker;*" and Marot's translation of the Psalms, "Marot's *sacred songs.*"

How triumphantly our controversial friends of the hymns can, by-and-by, quote Motley, the prince of historians, as proof that Huguenots and Hollanders sang hymns. How easy to turn, historically, the Psalms of the Bible into *modern hymns* of uninspired men!

Motley, in writing of these authors of translations and of their versions of the Psalms, and of their use by the French and Flemish churches, had not in his mind the technicalities of controversialists, and stayed not to make distinctions; but, in the language of his own New England, calls these authors and their versions of the Psalms—the one "the *hymn-book maker;*" the other, "Marot's *sacred songs,*" while really writing of French and Flemish versions of the Book of Psalms.

THE PALATINATE CHURCHES.

The following extracts from the *Mercersburgh Review*, written by Charles P. Krauth, D. D., may be seen in the *United Presbyterian* of April 14, 1870:—

"The original usage and tradition of the Palatinate Church was, that nothing *but the Psalms* and *the poetical parts of Scripture* should be sung in public worship. The Palatinate Church order says, expressly: 'Touching the singing of the *Psalms*, the Apostle Paul exhorts, etc., etc., wherefore it is our will that none other than the German *Psalms* be sung in our churches.' 'German *Psalms* shall be sung before and after the sermon.' 'If the people be able to sing, a penitential *Psalm* shall be sung.' . . .

"This book (spoken of in the first extract) has the Psalms rendered very closely, not with interpolations, changes of meaning, and subjective adaptations, like those of Dr. Watts, but rigorously as to the sense. It is the version of Lobwasser, the Rouse of the German Church. He was a Lutheran, but the rigid literalness of his renderings prevented their use in the Lutheran Church. The desire of the Reformed Church evidently was to have the Psalms as nearly like the original as was consistent with their being sung by the people. . . . To sing medications, like those of Dr. Watts and his school, as the very Psalms of David, would have been an abomination to the original Reformed Churches. . . . We speak advisedly when we say, that to the whole original Reformed Church, and especially to the Palatinate Fathers, a large proportion of what is sung as 'Psalms' in the English congregations of the German Reformed Church would have been intolerable, on the ground that, pretending to be Psalms of David, they were really the Psalms of Dr. Watts, and of the other authors of the sacred parodies. When the German Reformed Church came to use such imitations of the Psalms, she never put them among the Psalms, but where they belong, among hymns—human effusions suggested by divine originals. The other course is a complete confounding of the unequivocally apocryphal with the canonical, and the effect has been very mischievous. Dr. Watts' Psalms have virtually had the authority of inspiration with those who sing them."

It will require more historic evidence than is furnished by Mosheim, Neander, and all the copyists of Lutheran historians, to establish the hypothesis that the Apostolic Church — the Waldensian — the French Protestant and Huguenot — the Continental Reformed — the Scottish Presbyterian, were all hymn-singing churches; or, to establish as a historical truth, that with all these churches uninspired hymns were the rule, and inspired Bible songs the exception

HISTORY NOT THE RULE OF FAITH AND WORSHIP.

That uninspired hymns *may have been* introduced, as other heresies, in the third or fourth centuries, we are not very careful to deny. That such hymns were used in the worship of God, under the influence of the Roman apostacy, we do not pretend to deny. That Luther brought with him from Rome his love of hymns, as his love of consubstantiation, is too palpable to admit of denial. That Lutheran historians were even bigots for hymns, we are not inclined to deny. That they impartially represent either Presbyterianism or a Scripture psalmody, we are in no haste to grant. The Lutheran Church, in many things, was never much more than half reformed. While other Reformed churches were chanting the songs of the Bible, Lutheran churches were singing Lutheran hymns.

Lutheran historians sometimes prove nothing by attempting to prove too much; as, that Scripture Psalms were not sung in the Christian Church till the third or fourth century. Nobody believes this — not even those who quote and use the statement. And further, were more even than is well attested true, what could that settle in this controversy? Can any way of worship claim Divine authority because early and extensively practised in the Christian Church? Antichrist, that wicked one, began to work as early as the time of the beloved disciple John. His anti-Christian corruptions have been steadily working ever since, and are now, as ever, working, carrying the multitude, as on the bosom of a flood, with them. Are these corruptions therefore right? The same line of argument is used, and with better grace, by Arians, Baptists, Prelatists, and Papists. And will all their appeals to history and to the Fathers convert Presbyterians from their and our beloved, old apostolical and scriptural Presbyterianism? Never! And why? Simply because our home—the home of our dear Presbytery—is the Bible.

Before we shall, in this controversy, be affected by appeals to history, any more than in the controversy with Prelacy, our friends must furnish something more tangible, something more reliable, something more like *fact* and Bible teaching. We demand some author or authors of a hymn-book or hymn-books, some supreme judicatory or judicatories, which received, examined, approved, and authorized them to be sung in all the churches, and that were sung in all the churches during the first three centuries. We challenge even the shadow of authentic historical evidence that any poet prepared a book of hymns, that any apostolical supreme judicatory ever sat, or counselled, or deliberated, or adjudicated upon such hymn-book, or upon the adoption of any system of psalmody at all. More: we challenge authentic history for one single instance of the "Presbyterian way" of preparing hymns for the Church, outside the Papacy, for fourteen centuries from Christ. We demand the Watts of the Waldensian Church, his hymn-book, the approval and sanction of the Waldensian supreme judicatory, and the use of such hymn-book before the fifteenth century. So we demand of all the early Reformed Churches

—the Lütheran, of course, excepted. We are aware the Lutheran and all the other German Reformed Churches were at odds on the subject of the "*rigid literalness*" of the renderings of Lobwasser, the Rouse of the German Reformed Churches. There is more of authentic history and testimony bearing on the question of psalmody in the brief quotation from the "*Palatinate Order*"—the organic law and directory for worship of the Reformed Churches—than in all the scraps of Lutheran history, gathered and paraded mostly without satisfactory vouchers. There is, too, more evidence in the statements of Motley in regard to the Flemish version of Philip de Marnix for the use of the Reformed Churches—the French version of Marot, and the German of Lobwasser; for here are the translators, their tangible and veritable versions, the veritable churches and their organic law, settling the use of a Scripture psalmody. Where, till the time of Watts, among Reformed churches, the author, the hymn-book, the judicial sanction of any Reformed church in the modern Presbyterian way?

The inflexible tenacity of Luther was proverbial. His favorite motto, "*Hoc est meum corpus*," behind which he entrenched himself in battling for a darling heresy, was but the index to the man and his disciples, who so often betrayed their neutrality in the struggles of reformers with papal tyranny, or their sympathies with popish ritualism.

And then, what sin, heresy, error, or corruption in worship, cannot be proved venerable and hoary by history? Slavery has reigned for cycles of centuries; when, since the days of Nimrod, did it not curse the earth? Papal and prelatic corruption, ritualism, superstition, will-worship and tyranny have dominated over the masses—"the world wondering after the beast"—for twelve hundred years. Is all this, therefore, right, and of God? Rather, in stead, Christ's two witnesses are right, and their testimony approved of God, though wearing sackcloth, and in number as *two* to *one hundred and forty and four thousand* with the Lamb on the Mount Zion.

THE MISTAKE AND ITS FATAL TENDENCIES.

Our brethren object to our way of worship, because, as they charge, " it comes short of the New Testament pattern in some of the *fundamental doctrines* of the Gospel ;" and " our trumpet gives so uncertain a sound, our testimony for the great vital truth of Christianity is so vague and feeble, that Arians and Jews cordially hold communion with us. Can this be right? Where in the Psalms are we taught that the babe of Bethlehem was the child-born, the Son given of prophecy ?"

We are sorry to see here, as elsewhere, the inability of our brethren to see Christ in the Psalms *as he is really there.* We are sorry our friends cannot see Him as He saw and pointed others to Himself in them; that they cannot see Him as Apostles and inspired writers of the New Testament saw Him, and there point to Him so clearly in so many Psalms where neither His disciples nor we would have otherwise discovered Him. Brethren, we are aware that your cause and consistency demand that you see as little of Christ and of spirituality as possible in the Psalms. You need to have the veil of Moses or of prejudice well drawn over your minds when you read or sing the Psalms, lest you should see too much of Christ, of his fulness, and of their spirituality and richness; and lest you should feel the heart-warming power of His love and grace reflected from this part of His own perfect and transforming mirror. Such discoveries are always, and, necessarily, fatal to your cause. Though this may seem a hard charge, yet it is in *fact* true; for, *in fact* you endeavor to hide—pressed in debate by the necessity of your cause—Christ from yourselves and all others in the use of the Psalms. For example of *fact*, you lay Christ aside, put the veil over Him as He is in the *First Psalm;* because, assuming that Christ is not "that man of perfect blessedness, who walketh not astray"—as he is, primarily, *that* veritable man—you think you have a vantage ground; and so you assume it, and so improve it for the defence of your cause. You shut your eyes to the truth that no "*mere man*" is there described; that "no *mere man* since the fall," even for one day, failed to go astray in thought, word, and deed. So you cannot afford to have the Man of the *Twenty-fourth* Psalm to be the Man Christ, whose ascension we sing there—the Man of "*clean hands*" and "*pure heart;*" true of none but the Man who led captivity captive, and who is the King of glory. What else but this dreadful fatality could have led one of the champion defenders of your cause, in speaking of the Sixteenth Psalm, to use such expression as this: "This is plainly the sense, for how *could David's soul* (not his body) be left in the grave?" What, but some blind fatuity, induced by the spell of partisan controversy in a bad cause, could lead men, otherwise intelligent, to use such language in the very face of the positive declaration of holy writ, that the expression of the Psalm refers to the resurrection of Christ, and no more to David than to Adam? So, to subserve a bad cause, a veil must, as much as possible, be thrown over the Psalms to hide Christ from the faith of the worshipper.

Oh, how many precious Psalms, redolent with Christ, might we place in this category! But how painful! Rather, in what Psalm is there nothing of Christ? What one is not the very word of Christ? What one speaks not of His person, His work, His Gospel, His grace, or His hidden life.

Yes, brethren, we do find in the Psalms Christ, that Man

of "*perfect blessedness,*" that Man of "*clean hands* and *pure heart.*" We can find, too, that babe of Bethlehem, His birth and birthplace, His life, His sufferings, His death, His resurrection, His ascension, His glory and reign—all, all in the Psalms; and there delineated with a master's hand as human poet's pen can never do. And just here you or we are fatally mistaken. Do we find too much of Christ and His salvation in the Psalms? Are we in danger here of clinging too closely to the Bible songs to find and enjoy that measure of communion with our Saviour that we might by drawing from the effusions of uninspired poets? Can we, indeed, be in danger of finding too much spirituality in the inspired songs of Christ's own word?

Let me say, here, Christ is found in the Psalms, and of design, as in no other composition of the Bible. The Evangelists, as in no other part of the Bible, give the history of the outer man of Christ, as He was seen, and heard, and as He lived among men. The Psalms unfold His hidden life, the life of His soul—the hidden, inward, deep sorrows of the soul of the Man of sorrows, as no where else. Hear Himself speak the touching tones of the unutterable agonies of the inner soul:—

"Of death the cords and sorrows did about me compass round;
The pains of hell took hold on me; I grief and trouble found."

What sinner, under evangelical conviction for sin, can fail to find in this mirror the life-painting of the inner contrition and pangs of an awakened soul? And as Christ's inward experience as in the Psalms delineated—whether His sorrows, His joys, His faith or hope—is the perfect model of all Christian experience and of all gracious attainments, so His life there is presented as the perfect model of Christian life. As Christ never walked astray, as His hands were perfectly clean, and His heart perfectly pure, so *we should aim* and *must attain* before we shall appear with Him in glory.

Again, we think you here come in contact with an important Bible principle—to make a man an offender for a word which God in his word condemns. In the Psalms we have the *things* which you deny there, because the spirit of inspiration has not chosen the *words* that please you. We certainly find the birth of Christ in more Psalms than one, and according to prophecy the place, too, in words we understand; and, if you cannot so understand, we are sorry. We try to read and sing the Psalms of the Bible with the veil of Moses laid aside, which, perhaps, if you succeed in throwing off, you may discover the Christ in Bethlehem born in Psalm cxxxii. Instead of the old veil, we endeavor to read and sing with the new glasses of the New Testament on our eyes. We interpret our Psalms by the commentary of the New Testament. This we find to be the true key, and here we find the true glasses. Christ gave these glasses for the very purpose of the better seeing Him in the Psalms.

In regard to the very verbiage of the Psalms, it would seem they were clothed in terms designed to obviate the very objections pressed against their use. This fact is certainly remarkable everywhere in speaking of Christ—His birth, life, sufferings, death, resurrection, ascension, session at God's right hand—all as past; when to be, or yet to come? How much easier for us than for the Jews to sing in "literal form?" Moses' veil—with other veils—off, we can read their design for New Testament use especially, and most consistently sing, in very *words*, a Saviour *come*. Were the Psalms prepared specially for a dispensation lasting, after they were given, but a few hundred years, or for one of more thousands of years? Were they prepared for Jews or for Christians? In literal form, for which more literally appropriate? But Christ's Church is one. Praise, a moral duty, is one and unchanged by change of dispensation.

In bidding farewell to our readers, permit us to address a parting word to the friends of a Scripture psalmody.
Remember the importance of Bible knowledge. Remember Christ has said, "Search the Scriptures, for they are they which testify of me." Just in proportion as we study the word of God, just as we study to understand the teachings of the Psalms, so will we love them, so will we find Christ in them, so will we enjoy and profit by their use, finding in them food for our souls. Remember man shall not live by bread alone, but by every word which proceedeth out of the mouth of God. Whatever order or matter of worship will bring us into closer contact with the Divine mirror, that is the safest way of worship, bringing the greater glory to God, and the larger measure of enjoyment to ourselves. In the study and singing of inspired Psalms we bring our hearts under the direct influence of the reflecting and transforming power of that glass, beholding in which "we are changed into the same image from glory to glory, even as by the Spirit of the Lord." The Divine Spirit and Author of sanctification, we think, prefers to use His own mirror. We may be assured He will have respect to the Saviour's prayer: "Sanctify them through Thy truth; Thy word is truth." Can we doubt that the safer way is the use of Scripture songs, which we know, with unwavering confidence, have the approval of God; while we cannot have the same assurance that He approves the use of the erring effusions of uninspired erring men? "He that doubteth is damned if he eat." *Can* we, with the same confidence of faith, sing one thing as well as another? "Whatsoever is not of faith is sin." *Can* we

sing the songs of God's word in faith? *Certainly!* is the prompt answer of every believing heart. *Can* we as well sing in faith what man says—*man's words?* No man, fearing God, and believing His word as the only ground of faith, can, without trembling misgivings, at once respond, "*Certainly!*" Ah, how significant the contrast here! Yet, *certainly*, the language of the heart, inspired by faith and love to the Saviour, when the sound of the inspired song falls upon the ear, will be—" The voice of my Beloved! behold, He cometh leaping upon the mountains, skipping upon the hills." Such is the secret power of the *hand* of that " voice that knocketh" standing at the door,—a power that moves the heart and opens its foldings.

For Christian walk we have the counsel of unerring Wisdom here. Here we have the exhibitions of the life and character of the perfect Man, the Divine Man and mode' of Christian life and Christian attainments. Here is conspicuously set before us the Divine "*scopos*," the mark at which we must aim, and to which we must run. Here is revealed the hidden life and perfect model of Christian experience—the model test by which every grace and every exercise of grace can so satisfactorily and safely be tested. Here, too, is food for the soul, which, while it satiates, it never cloys nor tends to loathing; as honey, ever sweeter; as richest pastures, ever fresh and green; as crystal streams, never fouled; the bread and water, eating and drinking, we shall live upon and never hunger, never die. But when the dissolving time for this clay-house shall come, how believing instinct will turn to that Psalm made by our Shepherd's hand for the dying pillow! How many heads have rested there, and trembling hands have grasped the staff on which our Shepherd leaned.

"Yea, though I walk in death's dark vale, yet will I fear no ill;
For thou art with me, and *thy rod* and *staff* me comfort still."

Around these dear old songs, ever new, our affections cluster and linger. On these our faith has often rested, and our hope anchored. From these, in the dark hours of our pilgrimage, a cheering light has gleamed along our pathway, lightening up with brightness so often. We have seen our fathers pass along the dark valley, staying their steps down to the brink, and through the swellings of Jordan, with these as the Shepherd's staff in hand—these, the veritable covenant promises, all their salvation, all their desire. On these it is good to live; on these it is safe to die.

To my dear brethren in the ministry permit me to say:

Be not moved by the partisan cry of "Rouse's poetry, patchwork, paraphrase, no version at all." This is the last ditch in the controversial tactics of a bad cause. If our version have its blemishes, there is an easy remedy. Translations are human things. Our common Bible translation is a human thing, and has its full share of blemishes. We are not irrevocably pledged to any version of inspired songs. We demonstrate this by the verbal and rhythmical corrections of our old version, and by our endeavors to secure new and improved versions as we are able to add them, keeping steadily in view the integrity of translation and the literary demands of the age. We are not a stand-still Church in matters of mere form, or of taste, or of preference. In matters of faith, of Christian life and labors, of divinely instituted worship, let it be far otherwise with us. Let us ever walk with firm, unwavering step and faith into the sacred desk; there read, expound, and sing those precious songs of the divine psalter as our Master's text-book, inspired as every other book of the Bible is inspired. We know that with us it is not the preference of one hymn-book over another, or one version even exclusively.

We know, from comparison with the original text, the songs we sing in the public worship of God are His inspired word, if we have that word in our own language at all. With the text in our hands, before our conscience, in the presence of our flocks, and before the presence of our covenant God, we can roll back every challenge, whether from enemies without, or from unbelief within; we know and feel these songs to be the testimony of Jesus, the word of Christ, which He commands to let dwell in us richly, the ground of our faith, and His truth unchallenged. Are not these the Shepherd's pastures, where we should lead His flocks? And are not these the running streams of the water of life by which He would have us gently lead His lambs? Oh, these are healthier pastures; these are purer waters than those to which the flocks of the companions turn aside.

FRIENDS OF UNION: How long shall the sword devour? For the scathed tribes of Israel is there no gathering time? Faith brings her answer: "Zion's watchmen shall lift up their voice; with the voice together shall they sing; for they shall see eye to eye, when the Lord shall bring again Zion." Nothing more certain in the future than a union in the psalmody of the Churches. *Can* that be on the basis of any sectarian or denominational hymnology? *Why may* it not be on the songs of the Bible? *Could these* be offensive to any, or a stumbling block to anything but bigotry? Is there not matter enough in all the songs of the Bible for all the reasonable purposes of social praise? Are they not suitable? Are they not greatly superior to any hymnal extant, or any that man can make? Why, then, not unite where there can be a basis of union for all?

The Lord hasten it in His time! And to this end may the Lord bless our feeble reasoning together through these humble pages.

www.ingramcontent.com/pod-product-compliance
Lightning Source LLC
Chambersburg PA
CBHW022114160426
43197CB00009B/1017